OECD Reviews of Vocational Education and Training

Seven Questions about Apprenticeships

ANSWERS FROM INTERNATIONAL EXPERIENCE

OECD
BETTER POLICIES FOR BETTER LIVES

Please cite this publication as:
OECD (2018), *Seven Questions about Apprenticeships: Answers from International Experience*, OECD Reviews of Vocational Education and Training, OECD Publishing, Paris.
https://doi.org/10.1787/9789264306486-en

ISBN 978-92-64-30647-9 (print)
ISBN 978-92-64-30648-6 (pdf)

Series: OECD Reviews of Vocational Education and Training
ISSN 2077-7728 (print)
ISSN 2077-7736 (online)

Photo credits: © Designer things

Corrigenda to OECD publications may be found on line at: *www.oecd.org/publishing/corrigenda*.

Foreword

We live in a world where for too long, and in too many countries, vocational education and training (VET) has been the poor cousin of national strategies to provide young people and adults with the knowledge and skills they need – and employers demand. That is why vocational education has often been seen as a provision fit only for 'other people's children' against the gold standard of academic routes culminating in university study. But evidence from countries with high performing vocational systems tells us that they provide a very effective means of integrating learners into the labour market and for opening pathways for further learning and personal growth - and there are signs that things are changing.

A new wave of interest has emerged in response to rising concerns over both stubbornly high levels of youth unemployment and the unpredictability of the modern working world. Increasingly diverse and interconnected populations, rapid technological change in the workplace and in everyday life, and the instantaneous availability of vast amounts of information mean that work that can be automated or digitised can now be done by the most competitive individuals or enterprises, wherever on the globe they are located. Knowledge and skills have become the global currency of the twenty-first century, with a rising premium on those social and emotional skills that are best learnt at the workplace. So across the globe, governments are turning afresh to VET and introduced programmes aimed at enhancing its attractiveness. They aim to improve progression from VET into either skilled employment or higher level learning by harnessing the unique capacity of the workplace experience to develop skills of genuine value.

This new report builds upon landmark OECD studies into upper secondary VET (*Learning for Jobs*, 2010) and post-secondary provision (*Skills beyond School,* 2014) to focus attention on apprenticeships as a uniquely important form of work-based learning. Rooted in real life workplaces, apprenticeships actively engage employers to ensure the value of skills development, but more needs to be done to ensure high-quality experiences. The aim of this report is to lift the bonnet on the design of effective apprenticeship systems. Addressing fundamental questions like the duration of an apprenticeship and how much an apprentice should be paid, the report provides a framework for policy makers and practitioners working across the world. This synthesis report follows six focused studies which were generously supported by Australia, Canada, Germany, Norway, Scotland (United Kingdom), Switzerland, the United Kingdom (Department for Education, England/UKCES, UK Commission for Employment and Skills), and the United States and the European Commission.

This is an important time for vocational education. It is now widely accepted that the skills that are easiest to teach and test are also the skills that are easiest to digitise, automate and outsource. VET systems must rise to the challenge of this changing landscape if they are to remain relevant to the needs of learners and employers. This study furthers our ability to conceptualise and make sense of the changes now being encountered, enabling confident responses to emerging challenges. Looking forward, new data, including further results from the OECD's Survey of Adult Skills (PIAAC) and Programme of International Student Assessment (PISA), will help countries to compare the extent to which they have succeeded in ensuring that VET emerges as an attractive opportunity for all learners.

Andreas Schleicher,
Director for Education and Skills, and Special Advisor on Education Policy to the Secretary-General
OECD

Acknowledgements

Throughout this study, the OECD Secretariat has received essential guidance and support from the Group of National Experts on Vocational Education and Training and Adult Learning, with a particular debt to the chair, Stefan Wolter, and vice-chairs, Johan Uvin and Katalin Zoltán.

The analytical work on individual modules leading to this report was funded through voluntary contributions from Australia, Canada, Germany, Norway, Scotland (United Kingdom), Switzerland, the United Kingdom (Department for Education, England/UKCES, UK Commission for Employment and Skills), the United States and the European Commission. Switzerland, Scotland (United Kingdom), the United Kingdom and the United States hosted workshops, which provided valuable input into the work.

Particular thanks is owed to national co-ordinators, who commented on the draft working papers and provided background information. These include: in Australia, Rochelle Ball, Pat Donaldson and Juliet Zeiler; in Canada, Geneviève Babin, Marie Lavallée and Marie-France Chouinard; at the European Commission, Sigve Bjorstad and Mantas Sekmokas; in Germany, Oliver Diehl; in Norway, Benedicte Bergseng; in Scotland (United Kingdom), Tony Coultas; in Switzerland, Laura Antonelli, Paolo Bernasconi, Sarah Daepp, Marie-Laure Favre and Marlene Furrer; in the United Kingdom, Alison Morris; and in the United States, Johan Uvin and Sharon Lee Miller.

Within the OECD, Anthony Mann supported the preparation of this report as head of the Vocational Education and Training (VET) and Adult Learning team, with the OECD Centre for Skills, overseeing the final draft. Support throughout the exercise was received from Montserrat Gomendio as head of the Centre and from Deborah Roseveare and subsequently Dirk van Damme as head of the Skills beyond School Division.

This report draws heavily on working papers authored by Viktória Kis, Małgorzata Kuczera, Lucia Mýtna Kureková, Samuel Mühlemann, Pauline Musset and Hendrickje Windisch. Viktória Kis drafted Chapters 1 to 6. Pauline Musset drafted Chapter 7. Anthony Mann drafted the executive summary and overview. Tanja Bastianić provided statistical support throughout the exercise. Liz Zachary provided editorial support. Jennifer Cannon and Elisa Larrakoetxea prepared the text and steered the report to publication.

Table of contents

Tables

Figures

Boxes

Follow OECD Publications on:

http://twitter.com/OECD_Pubs

http://www.facebook.com/OECDPublications

http://www.linkedin.com/groups/OECD-Publications-4645871

http://www.youtube.com/oecdilibrary

OECD Alerts *http://www.oecd.org/oecddirect/*

This book has...

StatLinks

A service that delivers Excel® files from the printed page!

Look for the *StatLinks* at the bottom of the tables or graphs in this book. To download the matching Excel® spreadsheet, just type the link into your Internet browser, starting with the *http://dx.doi.org* prefix, or click on the link from the e-book edition.

Executive summary

After a period of relative neglect in many countries, apprenticeships and other forms of work-based learning are experiencing a revival, in recognition of their effectiveness in easing school-to-work transition and serving the economy.[1] The challenges, however, of engaging individuals, employers, social partners and education and training systems in such learning are significant. This synthesis report draws out policy messages on how to design and implement high-quality apprenticeships using material from the OECD project Work-based Learning in Vocational Education and Training. It draws on analytical work conducted throughout the project and policy messages set out in six published policy papers. It poses seven questions commonly asked by governments seeking to either introduce or reform apprenticeship systems for young people and/or older workers: 1) can apprenticeships provide a useful contribution in every country? 2) Should employers receive financial incentives for providing apprenticeships? 3) What is the right wage for apprentices? 4) How long should an apprenticeship last? 5) How can a good learning experience at work be ensured? 6) How apprenticeships can be made to work for youth at risk? and 7) How to attract potential apprentices?

Key findings

Analysis of apprenticeship systems around the world shows that central to effective provision is the simple realisation that apprenticeships will only work well if they are attractive to both apprentices and employers. Getting the cost-benefit balance right for both sides is essential for effective policy. While it is tempting for governments to provide financial subsidies to employers to take on apprentices, more productive approaches focus on influencing the balance of interests built into apprenticeship design. One size does not fit all, and the balance should reflect the type of apprenticeship and learner. Apprenticeship duration and apprentice wages should respond to the differing costs and benefits incurred. Attractive apprenticeships provide young people and adult learners with the prospect of long-term skilled employment. However, prospective apprentices often poorly understand what apprenticeships can offer, and it is a challenge for careers guidance services to ensure that young people have ample opportunity to fully understand apprenticeships before key decision points.

Key messages

Can apprenticeships provide a useful contribution in every country?

Interest in apprenticeships is growing across OECD countries. Whereas apprenticeships were once seen as a route for just a small proportion of learners in construction or the trades (such as plumbing or car maintenance), in a number of countries they have also become a route into administrative, managerial or professional employment in the public and third sectors as well as the private sector. The attractiveness of apprenticeship lies in their rare capacity to provide, with confidence, skills that are undoubtedly in demand in the labour market. At their best, apprenticeships clearly signal labour market relevance because they have been designed with employers and other social partners, and they are primarily delivered in real workplaces with real employers. High-quality apprenticeships offer a form of learning that is relevant across economies and countries. However, in order for them to flourish there must be fair competition between apprenticeships and alternative forms of education and training. No artificial incentives should undermine the relative attractiveness of apprenticeships. Equally, one size does not suit all in apprenticeship provision. It should be expected that the design features of apprenticeships (such as wage and duration) will vary by national and sectoral context to ensure that they are attractive to both employers and prospective apprentices. This variation reflects differences in the cost-benefit balance of the apprenticeship. The secret to rolling out apprenticeships is to get the balance right between the costs and benefits incurred by employers and apprentices. Tools now exist to help policy makers get this balance right.

Should employers receive financial incentives for providing apprenticeships?

The balance between costs and benefits is particularly relevant to discussions over whether employers should receive financial incentives to provide apprenticeships. There is certainly a strong case for public investment in apprenticeships – particularly where they are focused on providing young people with an educational launch pad for their working lives – but governments should be wary of universal tax breaks or subsidies aimed at employers. With the possible exception of well-designed and implemented employer-driven levy systems, governments would be better served by targeting funding at measures to increase how quickly apprentices develop skills and become fully productive. In other words, where there is employer resistance to apprenticeships, governments can intervene to tip the cost-benefit balance more in their favour. Measures such as actions to help improve the quality of in-company training and reducing administrative costs can make a difference and are especially important for smaller employers.

How much should an apprentice be paid?

The greatest cost incurred by employers is apprentice wages, and governments should take care to oversee a labour market that ensures pay is high enough to attract prospective apprentices, but low enough to reflect the fact that a significant proportion of the apprenticeship will be spent in unproductive tasks. This balance will vary between different types of apprenticeship and is best identified by sector or occupation through, for example, collective bargaining. Governments should consider setting a minimum wage to protect individuals from exploitation, and addressing additional financial barriers that might prevent apprenticeships from being attractive to older workers.

How long should an apprenticeship last?

Apprenticeship duration should reflect both the difficulty of skills being learnt and the characteristics of the learner. When the apprentice wage is low (below the marginal productivity of the apprentice), getting duration right is important to ensuring that apprenticeships are attractive: too short and employers lose out on the cost-benefit balance, too long and apprentices will be subject to exploitation. This is why the engagement of social partners is so positive in apprenticeship design: organisations representing employers and workers can argue out the optimal length of the programme of training. Attractive apprenticeships will, moreover, respond to the higher levels of skills and experience that older workers can be expected to bring with them. Countries have developed approaches to shorten the duration of apprenticeships for these learners. Such tools, when based on robust assessments, serve to build greater equity and efficiency into apprenticeship systems.

How to ensure a good learning experience at work?

On-the-job training is a critical element of any apprenticeship, but it cannot be taken for granted that employers will have the capacity to train well. Governments or social partners can require or encourage apprentice supervisors to undertake training themselves, and help managers to design work practices to maximise apprentice learning within productive tasks. Final apprenticeship examinations should recognise the importance of on-the-job training by going beyond tests for theoretical and technical knowledge and skills; for example, assessments should also address the fuller demands of the associated occupation, such as personal interaction or social skills. Simulations and role-playing exercises with examiners are innovative means of testing the full range of knowledge and skills required by an apprenticeship.

How to make apprenticeships work for youth at risk?

In many countries, apprenticeships are seen as a vehicle for improving outcomes for young people who have struggled to find employment or to continue in education after the completion of compulsory schooling. International evidence suggests that apprenticeship systems can help to make school-to-work transitions easier for such youth. While many countries offer employers subsidies to take on apprentices with weak academic profiles or from disadvantaged backgrounds, there is little convincing evidence of the efficacy of such financial incentives. More effective are interventions designed to increase the speed with which a "youth at risk" apprentice can become a skilled, productive worker, and so cover the costs incurred by employers in their training. These include changes to the standard duration of an apprenticeship, preparatory programmes to help make a young person more attractive to a recruiter, or personalised support to tackle problems encountered by an apprentice whilst undertaking the apprenticeship.

How to attract potential apprentices?

If apprenticeship systems are going to be successful, apprenticeships must be attractive to a wide range of young people. Attractive apprenticeships develop the knowledge and skills that employers demand and offer a genuine gateway to skilled employment. Where the quality of apprenticeships is poor, young people will "vote with their feet" and not participate. However, students and their families often have a weak understanding of what apprenticeships actually have to offer. This is particularly the case where apprenticeships are now available across a wide range of occupations at different skills levels. Career guidance services must ensure that young people make informed decisions at the right time. Evidence from the Programme for International Student Assessment (PISA) database has shown how career aspirations are shaped by gender, socio-economic status and migrant background. These aspirations rarely reflect labour market demand. There is an onus on schools to take a proactive and strategic approach to careers guidance which begins young, broadens ambitions, and ensures that regular encounters with independent and well-trained career guidance professionals are the norm. Essential to effective guidance is giving young people the chance to find out for themselves, through activities such as career talks and job shadowing, what it is like to follow different occupational and learning pathways, including apprenticeships.

Note

[1] Apprenticeships typically involve a structured mix of: 1) time spent at a workplace, during which apprentices develop skills and perform productive work; and 2) off-the-job training and education which is typically overseen by public authorities. In most countries, apprentices spend more than 50% of their time in the workplace. Apprenticeships lead to formal, nationally recognised qualifications.

Overview: Making apprenticeships work

Why look at apprenticeships?

One of the biggest challenges in developing skills for the labour market is to ensure that learning meets the needs of the workplace. One of the best ways of doing this is to make the fullest use of the workplace as a powerful learning environment, and to find effective mechanisms to link employer interest to the mix of training provision. After a period of relative neglect in many countries, apprenticeships and other forms of work-based learning are experiencing a revival, in recognition of their well-known effectiveness in easing school-to-work transition, but also increasingly because of their particular capacity to develop skills closely tied to labour market needs. Across the OECD moreover, there is a growing realisation that work-based learning is not simply relevant to manual or low-skilled occupations, but has an important role to play in responding to the emergence of new middle- and high-level skilled employment. Apprenticeships themselves are changing. Whereas once, it was suffice for an apprenticeship to develop a narrow set of technical skills, it is now necessary to cultivate broader skills, especially basic skills, to prepare resilient learners well placed to navigate the dynamic new economy. The challenges, however, of engaging individuals, social partners and education and training systems in such learning remain significant.

Background to this report

This report draws out policy messages on how to design and implement high-quality apprenticeships using material from the OECD project, Work-based Learning in Vocational Education and Training (VET) (Box 1). It draws on analytical work conducted throughout the project and policy messages set out in six published policy papers.

Work-based learning encompasses a range of formal and informal arrangements, including apprenticeships, informal learning on the job, internships and work placements of various types that form part of school-based vocational qualifications. Apprenticeships in particular have been in the spotlight in many OECD countries, not only in the aftermath of the Great Recession, but also following recovery. Many national and international initiatives illustrate great policy interest in the topic, such as the launch of the European Alliance for Apprenticeships and the creation of the Global Apprenticeship Network in 2013.

The scope of each module of the Work-based Learning in VET project was driven by policy priorities in funding countries and the availability of research evidence. This led to most modules focusing on apprenticeships, while some had a broader scope (for example looking at shorter episodes of work experience and other forms of workplace engagement as a tool for career guidance). In synthesising insights from the six modules, this report seeks to build a coherent set of policy messages that are enriched with relevant country examples of policy and innovative practice. To achieve this, the report uses a deliberately selective approach and focuses on apprenticeships, for which all six modules have yielded policy messages and country examples.

Box 1. The OECD project: Work-based Learning in Vocational Education and Training

The project was launched in 2015 in response to shared country interest in identifying policy responses to the challenges associated with achieving widespread use of high-quality work-based learning in vocational programmes.

The project consisted of six modules, each involving in-depth analytical work on a particular topic and an international workshop. Policy insights and supporting analysis were published in six policy papers:

- Striking the Right Balance: The Costs and Benefits of Apprenticeships.
- Incentives for Apprenticeship.
- Work, Train, Win: Work-based Learning Design and Management for Productivity Gains.
- Work-based Learning for Youth at Risk: Getting Employers on Board.
- Making Skills Transparent: Recognising Skills Acquired Through Work-based Learning.
- Working it Out: Career Guidance and Employer Engagement.

Australia, Canada, Germany, Norway, Scotland (United Kingdom), Switzerland, the United Kingdom (Department for Education, England/UKCES, UK Commission for Employment and Skills), the United States and the European Commission have provided voluntary contributions towards the work, either through sponsoring specific modules or contributing to the project as a whole.

All policy papers are available at: www.oecd-ilibrary.org.

How this report is organised

This report offers a comparative perspective on responses in policy and practice to the challenges that arise in the design and implementation of apprenticeships. It builds on comparative knowledge of VET systems across OECD countries developed through more than 40 country studies of VET conducted since 2007. Consequently, the report situates individual countries' apprenticeship policies and associated practices in the context of their own VET systems – with considerable variation across countries in the age and educational background of apprentices, occupations covered and pathways into and after apprenticeships.

This report focuses on seven essential questions that arise in the design of apprenticeship schemes and their effective implementation. The rationale for selecting these questions is to ensure an emphasis on areas where comparative analysis has greatest potential to add value. Countries signalled these areas as of high policy interest, and relevant international evidence was available through a combination of existing evidence and insights emerging from the work around the six modules of the Work-based Learning in VET project. This report is organised around the following seven questions and answers from international evidence:

1. Can apprenticeships provide a useful contribution in every country?
2. Should employers receive financial incentives for providing apprenticeships?
3. What is the right wage for apprentices?
4. How long should an apprenticeship last?
5. How to ensure a good learning experience at work?
6. How to make apprenticeships work for youth at risk?
7. How to attract potential apprentices?

Table 1. Published policy papers that feed into this report

Relevant policy papers
Kis, V. (2016[1]), "Work, train, win: work-based learning design and management for productivity gains", *OECD Education Working Papers*, No. 135, OECD Publishing, Paris, http://dx.doi.org/10.1787/5jlz6rbns1g1-en.
Kis, V. (2016[2]), "Work-based learning for youth at risk: Getting employers on board", *OECD Education Working Papers*, No. 150, OECD Publishing, Paris, http://dx.doi.org/10.1787/5e122a91-en.
Kis, V. and H. Windisch (2018[3]), "Making skills transparent: Recognising vocational skills acquired through work-based learning", *OECD Education Working Papers*, No.180, OECD Publishing, Paris, https://doi.org/10.1787/5830c400-en
Kuczera, M. (2017[4]), "Striking the right balance: Costs and benefits of apprenticeship", *OECD Education Working Papers*, No. 153, OECD Publishing, Paris, http://dx.doi.org/10.1787/995fff01-en.
Kuczera, M. (2017[5]), "Incentives for apprenticeship", *OECD Education Working Papers*, No. 152, OECD Publishing, Paris, http://dx.doi.org/10.1787/55bb556d-en.
Musset, P. and L Mýtna Kureková (2018[6]), "Working it out: Career guidance and employer engagement," *OECD Education Working Papers*, No. 175, OECD Publishing, Paris, https://doi.org/10.1787/51c9d18d-en.

Summary of policy messages

Chapter 1: Can apprenticeships provide a useful contribution in every country?

The challenges arising with apprenticeship implementation depend on contextual factors

There is wide variation across countries in the use of apprenticeships. Many countries seek to promote apprenticeships to facilitate school-to-work transition or to offer opportunities for adults to re-skill and upskill. Building apprenticeships in countries where apprenticeships are uncommon, or creating new programmes in economic sectors that typically rely on other forms of training, is challenging. However, some simple principles underpin effective provision:

- Social partners, notably professional bodies, should be involved in the design and implementation of apprenticeship schemes. This is essential to encourage their engagement with apprenticeships and ensure that programmes are suited to their needs and employers' capacity to provide placements.
- Competition between apprenticeships and alternative learning pathways (e.g. school-based programmes, post-secondary or tertiary education) needs to be fair.
- Apprenticeships are easier to implement where formal qualifications bring substantial benefits to the learner.

The design of apprenticeship schemes can be adapted to suit different contexts

There are many ways of organising apprenticeship schemes. The challenge is to identify an approach that works for both employers and learners. The country context matters, as do sectoral and firm characteristics, notably the size of the enterprise. The optimal design features (e.g. choices concerning wages, duration and funding) will often vary depending on these factors.

- The parameters of apprenticeship schemes can be adjusted to ensure that an apprenticeship is attractive to both employers and prospective apprentices.
- Analysing the costs and benefits of apprenticeships can inform the design of new schemes and the reform of existing schemes. Undertaking surveys to measure the costs and benefits of apprenticeships to employers can provide empirical evidence to inform policy making.

Chapter 2: Should employers receive financial incentives for providing apprenticeships?

Financial incentives to encourage employers to take on apprentices should be used with caution

There is a strong argument for governments to dedicate public resources to support apprenticeships, given the role of apprenticeships in preparing individuals for a job and a career, and the wider social benefits that apprenticeships yield. Many countries face the challenge of securing enough apprenticeship placements in firms. As a result, financial incentives have been widely used to encourage employers to offer more placements. Whether the use of financial incentives is desirable depends partly on the targeted policy objective.

Financial incentives may be offered to reward firms that recruit apprentices, in recognition of the fact that they shoulder a burden that would otherwise be carried by the state: the task of preparing young people for a career. This rationale may underpin incentives offered to all firms that take apprentices, regardless of the impact of the incentives on the provision of apprenticeship places.

However, international experience suggests that financial incentives should be used with caution and carefully evaluated.

- Universal incentives, which give all firms that take apprentices a fixed sum, have a small impact on firms' provision of apprenticeship places.
- Targeted incentives are designed to focus resources on placements that would not be offered in the absence of incentives: they may reward firms that take apprentices with certain characteristics (e.g. disadvantaged youth, disabled people) or be available only to certain sectors or types of firms (e.g. small firms). In theory, such incentives may have more impact, but they are costlier to implement and their effectiveness will depend on how precisely the scheme is designed. When targeted incentives are used, their impact should be carefully evaluated and compared to alternative tools (e.g. supporting training capacity in firms).
- Employers may have an interest in setting up a levy to share the costs of training between firms when the labour market is tight and it is hard to find skilled employees on the external labour market. Employers may also face a high risk that other firms will poach their fully trained apprentices. Money collected through a levy may then be used to offer incentives to employers taking on apprentices.

To encourage employers, governments should aim to improve the apprenticeship cost-benefit balance through system design, support and capacity building

Attention should focus on non-financial incentives that improve the cost-benefit balance to employers, such as readjusting the design of apprenticeship schemes and enhancing training capacity in companies. Governments and social partners can support smaller employers by:

- Encouraging employers to find ways to share the responsibilities and risks associated with the provision of apprenticeships.
- Promoting bodies that work with groups of small employers to co-ordinate training.
- Supporting small employers with the administration and provision of apprenticeships.

International evidence offers limited support for the use of financial incentives, but there are many other ways of making apprenticeships appealing to employers. Design features of apprenticeship schemes can be adjusted so that they work better for employers (as set out in Chapter 1), and these can be augmented by capacity-building measures that aim to support employers and get the best out of apprentices.

Chapter 3: What is the right wage for apprentices?

Apprentice wages should reflect the cost-benefit balance of different apprenticeships

Apprentice wages represent the largest share of the costs of apprenticeships to employers, so their level will impact firms' willingness to take on apprentices. Apprentice wages need to be set at a level that when all other costs (e.g. trainer's wages, training equipment and administrative costs) are included, employers can expect to recoup the total cost of apprenticeships through the productive work of apprentices and the prospect of recruiting the best apprentices as skilled workers.

Allowing apprentice wages to vary across occupations is desirable because the cost-benefit balance of apprenticeships to employers varies across occupations, and room for variation allows wages to help match supply to demand.

- Governments should not impose an overall level of apprentice wages, (although it may want to set a minimum wage to protect against exploitation) instead wage setting arrangements should allow for variation across sectors and occupations.
- Apprentice wages should gradually increase over the programme, as apprentices become more skilled and their productivity improves.

Apprentice wages should also reflect the characteristics of apprentices and policy priorities

Apprentice wages need to be low enough to encourage companies to offer apprenticeships, but high enough to attract apprentices. From the point of view of potential apprentices, the attractiveness of the apprentice wage depends on their needs and how the apprenticeship compares to alternative career pathways available to them.

- Where youth apprentice wages are low, governments should ensure that they are balanced by extensive benefits to the young apprentice in terms of the quality of the learning opportunities with the employer.
- When policy efforts aim to increase the use of adult apprenticeships, measures should be devised to ensure that the apprentice income is sufficient to make the apprenticeship affordable for adults. This should be based on analysis of the

relevant costs and benefits of particular target groups (e.g. by employment status and age) and may include financial support, on top of wages, for adult apprentices.

Chapter 4: How long should an apprenticeship last?

Apprenticeship duration should reflect the targeted occupation

Over the duration of an apprenticeship, apprentices need time to develop the targeted skillset, but once they have acquired those skills they have an interest in becoming a qualified skilled worker as soon as possible. Employers, on the other hand, need time to train apprentices on the job and put apprentices' newly developed skills to use by engaging them in productive work. This productive work, particularly in the later stages of an apprenticeship, typically compensates for employers' earlier investment into training. How long it takes to develop occupational skills and how those skills can be used in productive work varies across occupations.

- The duration of apprenticeships should be adapted to reflect the targeted occupation, in particular how apprentice productivity evolves during training.
- In occupations that target a more complex skillset and where more time is needed to master skills, a longer duration will be more appropriate.

Some flexibility in duration should be allowed to accommodate for different starting points and learning speeds of apprentices

Apprenticeship schemes are typically built around the needs of the main target population. However, some apprentices have a different background, for example, adults starting an apprenticeship in a country with a large youth apprenticeship system. The profile of the apprentice population within the same country can also change, for example through migration, creating a need to adapt schemes to the learning needs of apprentices.

Individuals who have some of the skills targeted by an apprenticeship programme can benefit from the possibility of adjusting the length of programmes to reflect some degree of prior learning. Policy options include:

- Encourage the possibility of accelerated completion to recognise that some adult apprentices already have many general and occupation-specific skills. This may be supported by creating framework conditions for apprentices with relevant work experience, rather than leaving everything to individual negotiations.
- Ensure that the package associated with shorter apprenticeships is attractive to both employers and apprentices.

Allow access to the final qualifying examination of an apprenticeship

Some individuals, particularly adults with relevant work experience or apprentice dropouts, will have most of the skills targeted by an apprenticeship programme and effective systems will respond to their higher levels of ability. For such people, even a shortened programme may seem too long. A more suitable path may involve topping up skills and filling in gaps through targeted preparatory courses prior to final apprenticeship examination. In those countries which allow direct access to examination without requiring participation in a full apprenticeship programme, participation rates are high.

Chapter 5: How to ensure a good learning experience at work?

The training capacity of employers must be built and supported

The quality of the learning experience in workplaces has a huge impact on the overall quality of apprenticeships, as apprentices spend much (and indeed, often most) of their time with an employer. But while schools are built around the objective of teaching, workplaces are designed primarily to produce. Taking on and training apprentices while continuing with day-to-day production activities is demanding for employers.

- Training capacity should be supported, helping employers to deliver high-quality training to apprentices. This support may be facilitated through public policy, through collective action by firms (e.g. sectoral bodies, employer organisations or unions) or a combination of both. Targeted training should be offered to apprentice supervisors.
- Stronger training capacity in workplaces benefits apprentices by ensuring that all have a high-quality learning experience at work, meaning that they can develop the technical and softer skills targeted by the programme that will equip them for successful careers.
- Employers can benefit by strengthening their training capacity through a better integration of apprentices into the production process. In firms that are better at training, apprentices develop skills faster. Where learning is better integrated into productive work, apprentices can practice and hone their skills, while also contributing to output.

Apprenticeship assessments must be rigorous

When an employer takes on an apprentice, it commits to develop the skillset targeted by the programme. Employers have some degree of autonomy over how they organise their apprentice's time on the job, as long as they cover that skillset. This autonomy needs to be balanced by rigorous assessments to check that all apprentices have developed the desired skills by the end of the programme.

One challenge is that occupations targeted by apprenticeships require a wide range of skills, including practical technical skills, which are often expensive to test directly, and soft skills (e.g. how to deal with an awkward client), for which traditional paper and pencil tests are poorly adapted. As a result, these aspects of the targeted skillset are often inappropriately assessed in examinations.

- Standards and procedures for assessment should be established to support clear and reliable qualifications. These should cover issues such as: what skills are assessed, how the assessment is conducted, and who will carry out the assessment. Mechanisms are necessary to ensure consistency in standards and in the use of the assessment in different parts of a country and at different points of time.
- Given the wide range of skills required by many occupations targeted by apprenticeships, assessments should incorporate, whenever possible, tests of the full range of skills required in the target occupation. These should include skills not adequately measured by traditional written and oral assessments, including practical technical skills and soft skills.

Chapter 6: How to make apprenticeships work for youth at risk?

Apprenticeship schemes need to be designed in ways that address the needs of youth at risk, while remaining attractive to employers

To realise the full potential of apprenticeships for youth at risk it is important to ensure that the prospect of taking on a young person at risk aligns with the business interests of enterprises. This requires shifting the balance of costs and benefits to employers to make it more attractive for them to offer opportunities to this group. International evidence suggests that this is best done through non-financial measures.

Changing the parameters of apprenticeship schemes (e.g. apprentice wages, duration, how apprentices' time is spent) can help make apprenticeships for youth at risk more attractive to employers. This may be implemented by:

- Creating a targeted apprenticeship scheme with a modified design that is suitable to the specific needs of youth at risk and is attractive to employers, for example, a shorter programme.
- Putting in place preparatory programmes (pre-apprenticeships) and support measures for youth at risk enrolled on regular apprenticeship schemes.

Youth at risk often need preparatory programmes to get them ready for an apprenticeship

When apprentices are well prepared, for example, they have caught up with any gaps in literacy or numeracy, have carefully chosen their target occupation and are ready to operate and learn in a real work environment, they will be more attractive in the eyes of potential employers and have more chance of completing their training. Many countries pursue extensive pre-apprenticeship programmes to this end.

- Pre-apprenticeship programmes encourage and offer financial resources to prepare youth at risk for apprenticeships.
- Given the diversity of approaches in this area, and the limited evidence base, new initiatives should be piloted and evaluated with the most effective programmes rolled out.

Youth at risk often require additional support over the duration of the apprenticeship

Youth at risk are more likely to drop out of an apprenticeship. This is likely to be to their own detriment and that of their employer. Dropout can be the result of both academic and personal difficulties. Consequently, youth at risk should be provided with additional support which might include remedial courses (e.g. in literacy and numeracy), mentoring and coaching. Employers should also be helped to build their capacity to provide apprenticeships for youth at risk. This might include support on how to handle difficulties that may arise with apprentices (e.g. through mediation), and how to put in place effective training for supervisors.

Chapter 7: How to attract potential apprentices?

Quality matters in making apprenticeships attractive

Achieving high-quality and high-status apprenticeships requires the creation of a virtuous circle in which investment in the quality of a programme leads to better employment prospects and earnings for the learner, which in turn attracts more high-ability candidates into the programme. This flow of high-ability students further improves the status of the programme and its attractiveness to employers, who will come to see it not only as high-quality education and training, but also as a means of recruiting able young students. This will further improve the labour market outcomes from the programme.

Career guidance is an essential feature of apprenticeship policy

Career guidance is both an individual and a social good: it helps individuals to progress in their learning and work, but it also helps the effective functioning of labour and learning markets and contributes to a range of social policy goals, including social mobility and equity. This justifies public investment in career guidance activities.

Strategic use of career guidance will broaden aspirations and challenge stereotypes

Effective career guidance services have a positive influence on the educational and employment outcomes of young people (Hughes et al., 2016[7]). The question of what makes career guidance effective has been considered by the OECD and other researchers extensively over the last ten years (Musset and Mytna Kurekova, 2018[6]). Some of the common challenges facing countries include the risks that career guidance is marginalised within school life, and that services are under-resourced and/or delivered by poorly trained staff who may lack objectivity and/or knowledge of the labour market (OECD, 2010[8]). Data from the Programme for International Student Assessment (PISA) show that it is often students who appear to have greatest need who have the least access to career guidance. For example, girls and students from low socio-economic status (SES) backgrounds often engage less frequently (Musset and Mytna Kurekova, 2018[6]).

Effective provision of career guidance should take into account the growing body of research literature and should:

- Provide regular opportunities for young people, from primary education onwards, to reflect on the relationship between their educational experiences and their prospective futures.
- Allow students to consider the breadth of the labour market, particularly occupations that are of strategic economic importance, newly emerging and/or likely to be misunderstood (such as the skilled trades).
- Undertake school-wide approaches that bring on board career guidance specialists, teachers and school leaders, and parents.
- Systematically engage people in work and workplaces.
- Provide easy access to trustworthy labour market information and advice from well-trained, independent and impartial professionals in advance of key decision points.
- Challenge gender and ethnic stereotyping.
- Target young people from the most disadvantaged backgrounds for the greatest levels of intervention.

Effective career guidance strategies demand close co-operation between schools and the world of work

To make properly informed decisions, students need to have a good picture of work and where they need to put their efforts while still in education in order to be able to realise their dreams. To achieve this, schools should encourage a first-hand understanding of the world of work from the earliest years.

Career guidance activities should fully integrate diverse members of the economic community into their career guidance services, ensuring multiple and authentic interactions with young people from an early age. Action should be taken to identify and address obstacles preventing engagement. Where countries are new to employer engagement, it is best to begin where logistics are easiest. In terms of delivery, countries and schools should consider that:

- Employer/employee talks and career fairs are a relatively easy and effective tool.
- Information and communication technology (ICT) can provide many new ways of facilitating the interactions between schools and employers.

References

Hughes, D. et al. (2016), *Careers Education: International Literature Review*, Education Endowment Foundation, London, https://educationendowmentfoundation.org.uk/evidence-summaries/evidence-reviews/careers-education/. [7]

Kis, V. (2016), "Work, train, win: work-based learning design and management for productivity gains", *OECD Education Working Papers*, No. 135, OECD Publishing, Paris, http://dx.doi.org/10.1787/5jlz6rbns1g1-en. [1]

Kis, V. (2016), "Work-based learning for youth at risk: Getting employers on board", *OECD Education Working Papers*, No. 150, OECD Publishing, Paris, http://dx.doi.org/10.1787/5e122a91-en. [2]

Kis, V. and H. Windisch (2018), "Making skills transparent: Recognising vocational skills acquired through workbased learning", *OECD Education Working Papers*, No. 180, OECD Publishing, Paris, http://dx.doi.org/10.1787/5830c400-en. [3]

Kuczera, M. (2017), "Incentives for apprenticeship", *OECD Education Working Papers*, No. 152, OECD Publishing, Paris, http://dx.doi.org/10.1787/55bb556d-en. [5]

Kuczera, M. (2017), "Striking the right balance: Costs and benefits of apprenticeship", *OECD Education Working Papers*, No. 153, OECD Publishing, Paris, http://dx.doi.org/10.1787/995fff01-en. [4]

Musset, P. and L. Mytna Kurekova (2018), "Working it out: Career guidance and employer engagement", *OECD Education Working Papers*, No. 175, OECD Publishing, Paris, http://dx.doi.org/10.1787/51c9d18d-en. [6]

OECD (2010), *Learning for Jobs*, OECD Reviews of Vocational Education and Training, OECD Publishing, Paris, https://doi.org/10.1787/9789264087460-en. [8]

Chapter 1. Can apprenticeships provide a useful contribution in every country?

This chapter explores the relevance of apprenticeship provision. It explores the universal benefits linked to the distinctive work-based character of apprenticeships, and finds considerable variation between countries in apprenticeship provision. The chapter identifies important elements that allow apprenticeships to work in the context of a given country, sector or occupation: the strength of social partnerships, the character of competition with alternative learning routes, and how entry to occupations is regulated. It also describes how apprenticeship schemes can be adapted to suit these different contexts. Finally, the chapter examines the costs and benefits of apprenticeships and how these can be adjusted to increase attractiveness to both employer and prospective apprentice, and how methodological tools enable such assessments to inform apprenticeship policy.

The statistical data for Israel are supplied by and under the responsibility of the relevant Israeli authorities. The use of such data by the OECD is without prejudice to the status of the Golan Heights, East Jerusalem and Israeli settlements in the West Bank under the terms of international law.

Issues and challenges

Apprenticeships have distinct advantages as a pathway to skills

Apprenticeships help connect provision in vocational education and training (VET) to labour market needs, as firms' willingness to offer placements provides an important signal of employer need for a particular occupation. They also make use of the powerful learning environment offered in workplaces. Apprentices can learn from employees who are familiar with the latest working equipment and techniques. Soft skills are an important part of the skillset in many occupations, and these are best learnt in real workplaces rather than in classrooms or simulated work environments (OECD, 2010[1]). For learners, apprenticeships are an attractive form of learning as they enhance skills in real life settings and prepare them for jobs and careers.

There is wide variation across countries in the use of apprenticeships

In some countries, apprenticeships are a well-established route to skilled employment, whereas in others, apprenticeships are uncommon, with employers favouring other means of training and upskilling their employees. Figure 1.1 shows the differences in enrolment in apprenticeships that lead to upper secondary or short post-secondary qualifications.

Figure 1.1. There are large differences in the use of apprenticeships

Current apprentices in programmes leading to upper-secondary or short post-secondary qualifications as a share of all students enrolled in upper-secondary and short post-secondary education

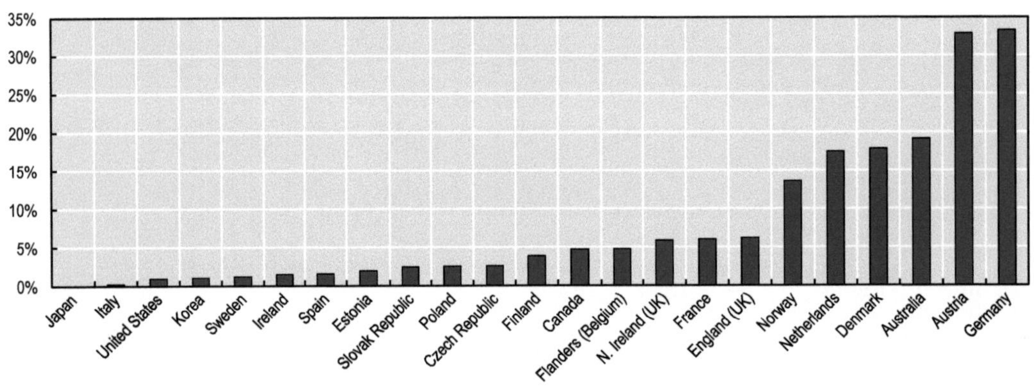

Note: 16-25 year-olds pursuing a programme at ISCED 3 and ISCED 4C level.
Source: Kuczera, M. (2017[2]), "Striking the right balance: Costs and benefits of apprenticeship", *OECD Education Working Papers*, No. 153, http://dx.doi.org/10.1787/995fff01-en.

StatLink http://dx.doi.org/10.1787/888933828372

The potential of apprenticeships is often underexploited for the jobs of the future

The popular image of an apprentice is often of working in a skilled trade or craft, such as construction or manufacturing. This accurately reflects the apprenticeship landscape in many countries, where apprenticeships are most common in manufacturing, construction and engineering. In the United States, for example, approximately 50% of apprentices are in the construction sector and 25% in military occupations (DOL, 2018[3]). One challenge is that the concentration of apprenticeships in skilled trade and craft occupations constrains apprenticeships to a small part of the labour market. In recent decades, OECD economies have seen a shift in employment away from manufacturing and towards services, which now account for over two-thirds of employment on average (OECD, 2017[4]). Limiting apprenticeships to "traditional sectors" means missing out on the potential benefits of apprenticeships in sectors where most of tomorrow's jobs will be found.

Countries with large apprenticeship systems have expanded beyond trade and craft occupations. Australia now has more non-trade than trade apprenticeship starts. In Switzerland, the three most popular apprenticeship occupations are business and administration, wholesale and retail sales and building and civil engineering (Federal Statistics Office (FSO), 2018[5]). In Germany, the most popular apprenticeship occupations are in the management and retail sectors (BIBB, 2017[6]). In Austria, office, trade and finance is the second largest group of apprentice occupations, with nearly as many apprentices as the machine and metal sector (Wirtschaftskammer Österreich (WKO), 2018[7]). In the United Kingdom, it is possible to pursue an apprenticeship as a policy adviser in the civil service (GOV.UK, 2016[8]).

A focus on traditional trades limits work-based learning opportunities for women

Skilled trade and craft occupations are often perceived as traditionally "male" with limited female participation. As a result, women seeking a vocational qualification mostly pursue school-based programmes and do not benefit from the advantages of apprenticeship schemes. For example, in the United States only one in five apprentices are female (DOL, 2018[3]). In Ireland, apprenticeships were similarly construction dominated until recent reforms. In 2004, women accounted for less than 1% of new apprentices, but three-quarters of those pursuing school-based VET (Watson, McCoy and Gorby, 2006[9]). One way of addressing the gender imbalance that emerges in such "traditional" apprenticeships is to encourage women to enter traditionally male occupations. Several countries have implemented tools to encourage this, but large differences persist in the occupational choices of men and women. This suggests that addressing the gender imbalance also requires the creation of apprenticeship programmes in fields that tend to attract many female applicants.

International experience shows that apprenticeships can be introduced in non-traditional fields

In recent decades, many countries have sought to diversify the sectoral coverage of apprenticeships in recognition of the potential of apprenticeships as a pathway to a wider range of skilled jobs. Australia introduced non-trade apprenticeships[1] in the 1980s, and these now outnumber trade apprenticeships (Hargreaves, Stanwick and Skujins, 2017[10]). In England (United Kingdom) and Ireland, apprenticeships used to be mostly in traditional trade fields, but service sector apprenticeships have grown strongly in England (United Kingdom) since the 1990s (Lanning, 2011[11]), and Ireland introduced programmes in service and business areas following the economic crisis (Condon and Mcnaboe, 2016[12]).

There are many ways of organising apprenticeships

Apprenticeship models, defined in law through agreements with employers and sometimes labour representatives and embedded in custom, differ across countries. For example, how on-the-job and off-the-job components alternate varies: in Austria, Germany and Switzerland, they are typically alternated within a week; in Ireland in blocks of several weeks; and in Norway, a two-year long school-based component is followed by two years spent in the workplace. Apprentice pay is also highly variable, with apprentices earning a very small share of a skilled wage in some countries and a much higher share in others (see Table 3.1 in Chapter 3). The status of apprentices also varies: in Germany, Norway and Switzerland, apprentices have a special contract, and terminating that contract ends the relationship of the apprentice with the employer; whereas in England (United Kingdom), apprentices are considered employees and sign an apprenticeship agreement on top of an ordinary contract.

The challenge for policy makers is to design schemes that suit a given context

Cross-national differences in the design of schemes affect how attractive apprenticeships will be for potential apprentices and employers, as well as how it will affect public finances. The challenge for policy is to develop apprenticeship schemes that work in the context of a given country, sector and occupation. This requires a closer look at the costs and benefits of apprenticeships, which is in the focus of policy argument 1 below. Chapters 2 to 6 focus on various questions that arise in the design of apprenticeship schemes.

The challenges arising with apprenticeship implementation depend on contextual factors

There is wide variation across countries in the use of apprenticeships. Many countries seek to promote apprenticeships to facilitate school-to-work transition or to offer opportunities for adults to re-skill and upskill. Building apprenticeships in countries where apprenticeships are uncommon or creating new programmes in economic sectors that typically rely on other forms of training is challenging. However, some simple principles underpin effective provision:

- Social partners, notably professional bodies, should be involved in the design and implementation of apprenticeship schemes. This is essential to encourage their engagement with apprenticeships and ensure that programmes are suited to their needs and employers' capacity to provide placements.
- Competition between apprenticeships and alternative learning pathways (e.g. school-based programmes, post-secondary or tertiary education) needs to be fair.
- Apprenticeships are easier to implement where formal qualifications bring substantial benefits to the learner.

Contextual factors affect how desirable apprenticeships are likely to be for employers and potential apprentices. They also affect how hard or easy it may be to carry out the implementation of apprenticeship programmes, such as agreeing a framework that sets out the content of programmes and how they are delivered, and ensuring their quality. Some of the factors identified concern differences between countries, whereas others are specific to sectors or occupations.

Policy argument 1: Strong social partnership facilitates the implementation of apprenticeships

Social partner involvement helps establish the core content of programmes

Employers are in a strong position to see if qualifications and curricula meet current labour market needs. They can also guide their adaptation to changing requirements. Apprenticeships are different from many forms of employer-led training as they prepare for an occupation and a career. To achieve this they must contain a large share of strong core content and develop skills specific to the occupation and sector. This is easier to achieve in sectors and occupations where employers (and often unions) are well represented and organised (see Box 1.1 for country examples). Defining the core content of each apprenticeship programme requires taking into account the diverse opinions of employers. *Ad hoc* consultative arrangements may give undue influence to a few random (often larger) companies (OECD, 2010[1]). At the same time, sometimes employers have incentives to create apprenticeships that narrowly fit a niche sector. However, although such programmes may be of interest of employers, they may create an artificial barrier to labour mobility as they disguise or develop few skills that are transferable to other occupations (Kuczera and Field, 2018[13]). Trade unions can usefully balance the influence of employers and champion interest in transferable skills. In some apprenticeship schemes, trade unions lead the development and running of apprenticeships (e.g. union apprenticeships in the United States).

Box 1.1. Social partners in apprenticeship policy development

Norway

Social partners (employers and trade unions) play a very active role in policy development at national, regional (county) and sectoral levels. The National Council for VET advises the Ministry of Education on the general framework of the national VET system. The Advisory Councils for VET are linked to the nine vocational programmes provided at upper-secondary level, and advise national authorities on programme content and future skill needs. The county vocational training committees advise on quality, provision, career guidance and regional development.

Source: Kuczera, M. et al. (2008[14]), *OECD Reviews of Vocational Education and Training: A Learning for Jobs Review of Norway 2008*, http://dx.doi.org/10.1787/9789264113947-en.

Switzerland

The apprenticeship system is steered at the national level by the Confederation, the cantons and professional organisations (employers, trade associations and trade unions). This arrangement is stipulated by law. The Confederation ensures quality and strategic planning and development of programmes, while 26 cantonal agencies implement and supervise apprenticeship programmes. Professional organisations establish the course content and develop qualifications and examinations and have an important role in the provision of VET by encouraging employers to offer apprenticeship places.

Source: Hoeckel, K., S. Field and W. Grubb (2009[15]), *OECD Reviews of Vocational Education and Training: A Learning for Jobs Review of Switzerland 2009*, http://dx.doi.org/10.1787/9789264113985-en.

Social partnership facilitates the delivery of high-quality training

Firms in sectors that have strong social partnerships have access to training know-how and institutional support not available to companies from other sectors and occupations. For example, training offices in Norway are owned collectively by firms and help the delivery of training by establishing new apprenticeship places, training apprentice supervisors and organising theoretical training for apprentices (Kuczera et al., 2008[14]). In Germany, chambers organise inter-company training centres, which complement training undertaken at school and within individual firms (BIBB, 2018[16]). Similarly, in Switzerland, professional organisations run courses in third-party training centres in most occupations, in addition to developing course content and training plans (FDEA, 2008[17]).

Policy argument 2: Apprenticeships face competition from alternative pathways to skilled jobs

Apprenticeships often compete with school-based programmes

Apprenticeship is typically one of several pathways to skills and skilled jobs. When offered at upper secondary level, young people may have a choice between academic or school-based vocational programmes. For example, research found that in Austria, apprenticeships compete with school-based vocational programmes (driving up apprentice wages, as discussed in Chapter 3). Meanwhile in Switzerland, school-based vocational alternatives are less readily available, so the apprenticeship system faces little competition (Moretti et al., 2017[18]). Apprenticeship schemes that build on completed upper secondary education compete with post-secondary and tertiary education.

The nature of competition depends on the country context

In some education systems, young people are tracked into pathways depending on their school results, so choices may be limited to which kind of apprenticeship programme to pursue. At the other extreme, such as in Israel, an apprenticeship is in effect a second chance pathway for school dropouts, rather than a genuine option for young people (Kuczera, Bastianić and Field, 2018[19]). In countries where post-secondary and tertiary education requires paying sizable tuition fees, apprenticeships may be financially attractive (e.g. as in England [United Kingdom] and the United States). Sometimes, ensuring fair competition between apprenticeships and alternative options is a challenge. When apprentices are not entitled to the financial support offered to those pursuing other pathways, competition becomes biased. For example, a recent OECD study of England (United Kingdom) noted that young apprentices are treated as employees and are not entitled to social benefits offered to those in school-based programmes.

Employers also consider apprenticeships among other options

For employers too, apprenticeships are often one of several ways of training and recruiting skilled employees. Firms may see few reasons to offer apprenticeships if publicly funded vocational programmes provide a pipeline of skilled workers. They may prefer to hire unskilled workers and train them on the job or employ graduates of school-based programmes and top up their skills with training.

Apprenticeships must be of high quality to compete with alternative pathways

Beyond the immediate financial implications of different pathways, individual choices (and parental preferences) depend on the prospects that people feel they offer. Individual preferences and employer preferences can be part of a vicious cycle – or a virtuous one. If apprenticeships are of poor quality, employment outcomes for apprenticeship graduates will be weaker. For young people, apprenticeships then become a second choice and those who can, will pursue other options. With apprenticeships of poor quality, employers cannot rely on them as a proof of strong occupational skills, so it makes sense for them to prefer graduates of school-based programmes or those with a post-secondary or tertiary qualification. However, the cycle can also be virtuous: high-quality apprenticeships where apprentices develop useful occupational skills, which are reflected in credible qualifications, will lead to good employment outcomes. For individuals considering different options, an apprenticeship then becomes an attractive pathway to skills; and for employers, it becomes an attractive way of securing a skilled workforce. Chapters 2 to 6 focus on the challenges that arise with designing and implementing high-quality apprenticeships, and how they may be addressed.

Box 1.2. A European Union approach to high quality apprenticeships

The Council of the European Union adopted a Recommendation on a European Framework for Quality and Effective Apprenticeships (EFQEA) on 15 March 2018.

The overall objective is to increase the employability and personal development of apprentices and to contribute to the development of a highly skilled and qualified workforce, responsive to labour market needs. The specific objective is to provide a coherent framework for apprenticeships based on a common understanding of what defines quality and effectiveness, taking into account the diversity and traditions of VET systems and policy priorities in the various Member States.

The Framework outlines 14 criteria for quality and effective apprenticeships: 7 for learning and working conditions and 7 for framework conditions.

Member States have three years to implement the Framework.

Source: EUR-Lex (2018[20]), *Council Recommendation of 15 March 2018 on a European Framework for Quality and Effective Apprenticeships*, https://eur-lex.europa.eu/legal-content/EN/TXT/?uri=CELEX:32018H0502(01).

Policy argument 3: Strong occupational regulation and employment protection make qualifications more important

Among the many forms of work-based learning, apprenticeships are special as they lead to a recognised qualification. The importance of holding a recognised qualification depends on the occupation and whether it is regulated: in regulated (or licensed) occupations, only those holding a specific qualification are allowed to practice.

Apprenticeships are easier to implement in regulated occupations

With a regulated occupation, the qualification delivered at the end of an apprenticeship is essential for both individuals considering pathways to skills and for employers in search of suitable employees. Without the qualification, skills learnt on the job would be of little use, as a skilled but unqualified person would not be allowed to work. However, in non-regulated occupations, other types of work-based learning may suit both learners and employers – an initially unskilled employee might pick up skills on the job and relevant work experience may be enough to prove their skills and progress throughout their careers.

Another factor that facilitates the implementation of apprenticeships is that the required qualification for an apprentice in a regulated occupation clearly sets out what is expected of a qualified person. Where occupational standards in terms of content are already explicitly or implicitly agreed in the labour market, apprenticeship programmes can build on these standards. This commonly agreed core skillset is at the heart of apprenticeship programmes – they ensure that, for example, an apprentice logistician in one firm develops the same core "logistician skillset" as those training in other firms.

The extent of occupational regulation varies across countries

Countries (and sometimes regions within a country) vary a great deal regarding which occupations require a particular qualification to practice (Koumenta et al., 2014[21]). Regulation is widespread in occupations where there are compelling health or safety concerns (e.g. electrician, occupations in healthcare), but some countries regulate access to occupations such as car mechanic, florist or manicurist, while others do not.

Collective agreements sometimes create qualification requirements

Sometimes, collective agreements established between social partners specify access requirements to a job or regulate promotion criteria, making a specific qualification necessary to reach the next step in the career ladder. The practical implications are similar to those of occupational regulation: a specific qualification will be necessary to fully pursue a career in the occupation concerned.

Employers are more likely to expect a relevant qualification when firing is hard

Stringent employment protection makes initial recruitment riskier for employers, because of the difficulty or cost of firing those who turn out to not be suited to the job. When regulation is most stringent for permanent jobs, employers may be particularly demanding when hiring. Research suggests that when employment protection is stringent, firms have higher hiring standards (Blanchard and Landier, 2002[22]; Kahn, 2016[23]), often in the form of expecting a given qualification (Breen, 2005[24]). Research also suggests that qualifications play a particularly important role in signalling people's skills in countries with larger VET systems, and where schools and employers have close links (Breen, 2005[24]).

The design of apprenticeship schemes can be adapted to suit different contexts

There are many ways of organising apprenticeship schemes. The challenge is to identify an approach that works for both employers and learners. The country context matters, as do sectoral and firm characteristics, notably the size of the enterprise. The optimal design features (e.g. choices concerning wages, duration and funding) will often vary with these factors.

- The parameters of apprenticeship schemes can be adjusted to ensure that apprenticeships are attractive to both employers and prospective apprentices.
- Analysing the costs and benefits of apprenticeships can inform the design of new schemes and the reform of existing schemes. Undertaking surveys to measure the costs and benefits of apprenticeships to employers can provide empirical evidence to inform policy making.

Policy argument 1: Employers will offer apprenticeships if benefits exceed costs

Employers can obtain benefits during the apprenticeship programme

Employers will normally provide apprenticeships when they believe that the benefits outweigh, or are at least equal to, the costs (Table 1.1 sets out the main types of costs and benefits to firms). The benefits emerge through two potential channels. First, during the apprenticeship apprentices can contribute to production, initially performing unskilled tasks and gradually undertaking more and more skilled tasks. Second, employers obtain benefits when the apprentice performs those tasks at a lower cost than a regular employee would do.

During apprenticeships, employers bear various costs

Apprentice wages typically represent the largest part of costs to employers (Chapter 3 focuses on apprentice wages). Other pay-related costs include, for example, social security contributions and the reimbursement of travel costs. The second largest cost is usually the cost of apprentice supervisors: skilled employees who spend time away from work to train and guide apprentices. One small research project in Flanders (Belgium) found that the main apprentice supervisors spend a third of their time looking after apprentices (De Rick, 2008[25]). Supervisor costs account for 38% of costs in Switzerland and 23% of costs in Germany (Strupler, Wolter and Moser, 2012[26]). Further costs for employers arise from paying for tools and equipment used by apprentices. Offering apprenticeships also involves administrative costs.

After the end of an apprenticeship, employers can reap benefits through recruitment

The second channel of potential benefit relates to longer-term returns. Upon completion, employers can select reliably productive apprentice graduates, rather than hire employees from the external market. Recruiting former apprentices means the company saves recruitment costs as they do not need to pay for job advertisements or organise interviews, and the company's former apprentices can skip much of the initial training that external recruits need (Mühlemann and Leiser, 2015[27]). Retaining a former apprentice as a skilled worker also minimises the risk of wrong recruitment, as the employer will know how the person performs at work – something much harder to judge when considering external candidates. In addition, once a former apprentice is recruited, the company might choose to pay them a wage slightly below their productivity, because they have privileged knowledge of their performance (Acemoglu and Pischke, 1999[28]). Such "recruitment benefits" are a major factor in motivating firms to provide apprenticeships in many occupations and countries.

Table 1.1. Types of costs and benefits to firms

Costs	Benefits
Apprentice wages and related costs (e.g. travel costs, food allowance)	Productive contribution of apprentices through unskilled tasks
Apprentice supervisor costs	Productive contribution of apprentices through skilled tasks
Training material and infrastructure, supplies (e.g. tools, software, books)	Recruitment benefits (e.g. savings on hiring costs, lower turnover)
Recruitment and administrative costs	Better reputation, social responsibility

Source: Adapted from Mühlemann, S. (2016[29]), "The cost and benefits of work-based learning", *OECD Education Working Papers*, No. 143, https://doi.org/10.1787/5jlpl4s6g0zv-en.

Policy argument 2: Parameters of apprenticeship schemes can be adjusted to improve the cost-benefit balance

Several factors that affect the cost-benefit balance to employers can be subject to policy influence

Chapters 2-6 discuss in detail how the following factors influence the provision of apprenticeships and present related policy messages:

- **Apprenticeship duration**: Initially, apprentices tend to contribute little to productive work, and often cost more than they produce. However, at the final stages, apprentices can contribute to production with their skills but are still cheaper than skilled workers, which can allow employers to reap net benefits.
- **How an apprenticeship is organised**: While apprentices are off the job they develop job-relevant skills, but do not contribute to production. What exactly apprentices do while on the job is also important: productive work always benefits employers, whereas learning activities bring benefits later when apprentices use their newly learnt skills to work. With care, learning can often be integrated into productive work, yielding higher benefits for firms.
- **Incentives**: Firms may receive subsidies or benefit from tax breaks when they take on an apprentice. Some incentives may be non-financial, like linking the award of public procurement contracts to the provision of apprenticeships.
- **Apprentice wages:** Representing the largest share of costs to employers, how apprentice wages are set, and their amount, have a strong impact on the cost-benefit balance. While policy makers typically do not set apprentice wages, policy tools can influence them.
- **Apprentice characteristics**: Apprentices with stronger skills will be more productive throughout the apprenticeship than those with weaker skills, and will generate higher benefits for the employer.

The design of schemes can be adjusted to contextual factors

Some factors are part of the broader context and are not directly influenced by apprenticeship policy. They also affect the cost-benefit balance to employers and need to be taken into account when setting the parameters of apprenticeship schemes. These factors include:

- **Wage context**: Apprenticeships will be financially more appealing for employers if there is a large difference between the wages of apprentices and those of skilled workers. Minimum wage laws and collective bargaining agreements are often important as they affect the wage costs of workers and apprentices.

- **Labour market features**: There will be more room to reap "recruitment benefits" if hiring in the external labour market is hard and expensive. This is the case when the labour market is tight, so jobs are abundant and relatively few people are in search of a job (Mühlemann and Leiser, 2015[27]). Employment protection is also important: when it is costly to fire a recruit who turns out to be a poor choice, an apprenticeship can be a good way of reducing the risk of wrong recruitment.
- **Occupation**: How long it takes for an apprentice to become proficient at a job varies across occupations, as does the cost of equipment involved, so the cost-benefit balance during apprenticeships varies. Potential "recruitment benefits" also vary: hiring costs tend to be higher in jobs that require sophisticated technical skills (Mühlemann and Leiser, 2015[27]).
- **Firm size**: The cost-benefit balance during apprenticeships varies with firm size: larger firms exploit economies of scale (e.g. training several apprentices on the same equipment), and sometimes have better opportunities to train apprentices while involving them in production. On the other hand, larger firms tend to train more in technical occupations (with higher training costs) than smaller firms, which often hire apprentices in the crafts sector. Larger firms are more likely to realise "recruitment benefits" as they tend to face higher hiring costs and more often recruit their apprentices as skilled workers (Mühlemann, 2016[29]).

The attractiveness of an apprenticeship to potential apprentices depends on various factors

The apprentice wage and labour market prospects affect the attractiveness of apprenticeships to young people or adults considering training options. When apprenticeships are more attractive, employers will have a greater pool of better prepared and skilled applicants, and a lower risk of costly dropout.

Policy argument 3: Empirical evidence on costs and benefits can underpin policy choices

Data reveal a great deal of variation in the cost-benefit balance of apprenticeships to employers

Empirical evidence shows that the cost-benefit balance varies across countries and across firm types and occupations within countries. Surveys have been conducted in Germany and Switzerland, and more recently in Austria (see Box 1.2), which reveal major differences between these three countries, which all have a long-standing tradition of apprenticeships. For example, an average Swiss firm generates a net profit, while an average firm in Austria and Germany incurs net costs while providing apprenticeships (Dionisius et al., 2008[30]; Moretti et al., 2017[18]). In terms of compensation for investments during apprenticeships, both Austrian and German companies are more likely to retain their apprentices as skilled workers, thus reaping benefits from recruitment (Mühlemann, 2016[29]; Moretti et al., 2017[18]). Austrian firms also receive subsidies. Within countries, empirical evidence reveals variations in the cost-benefit balance across firm types and occupations (see for example Figure 2.1 in Chapter 2).

Box 1.3. Cost-benefit surveys of apprenticeship

Cost-benefit surveys of apprenticeships have been conducted in relatively few countries. The initial methodology was proposed in the 1970s in Germany. The first surveys focused on costs, while subsequent surveys also covered benefits during apprenticeship, and later post-training benefits. In Switzerland, the first representative survey was conducted in 2000 using a very similar methodology to that used Germany. This was followed up by surveys in 2004 and 2009. In Austria, a cost-benefit study was conducted in 1997 with a different methodology, but the latest survey in 2016 used the same methodology as Germany and Switzerland.

Estimating benefits during apprenticeships

Supervisors who work daily with apprentices in the workplace are asked to estimate the fraction of time that apprentices perform unskilled and skilled work. The benefit from unskilled work equals the number of hours an apprentice spends performing unskilled tasks, multiplied by the wage of an unskilled worker within the training firm. The same principle applies for skilled work; however, the value to the firm is adjusted by the apprentice's relative productivity in skilled tasks (e.g. if an apprentice takes two hours to carry out a skilled task that a skilled worker would complete in one hour, the relative productivity of the apprentice will be 50%).

Estimating costs

The largest cost element is apprentice wage and related costs (e.g. bonuses, 13th month salary and subsidised lunch). The second main cost is the labour costs for apprentice supervisors: firms were asked to report the number of instruction hours that prevented supervisors from carrying out their regular duties in the workplace. When firms hire external instructors to teach certain skills at the workplace, the costs generated were also included. Other costs measured by the surveys include equipment or materials solely for apprenticeship training, and diverse costs such as tuition fees for external courses, books or learning software.

Source: Moretti, L. et al. (2017[18]), "So similar and yet so different: A comparative analysis of a firm's cost and benefits of apprenticeship training in Austria and Switzerland", *IZA Discussion Paper Series*, No. 11081, http://ftp.iza.org/dp11081.pdf; Mühlemann, S. (2016[29]), "The cost and benefits of work-based learning", *OECD Education Working Papers*, No. 143, https://doi.org/10.1787/5jlpl4s6g0zv-en.

Empirical evidence can help assess the implications of policy choices

Empirical evidence can be used to simulate different scenarios and inform choices regarding different parameters of apprenticeship schemes, for example, higher or lower apprentice wages, or changes in time spent in the workplace or in tasks performed by apprentices. For example, Moretti et al. (2017[18]) argue that if apprentice wages in Austria were set like those in Switzerland, and Austrian apprentices spent as much time at work as Swiss apprentices, an average Austrian firm would generate net benefits during apprenticeships.

Some studies have used apprenticeship data from countries where cost-benefit surveys have been conducted and combined these with contextual data (e.g. wages of skilled and unskilled workers) from another country. For example, a study using Swiss data in the context of VET in Spain (Wolter and Mühlemann, 2015[31]) concluded that three-year programmes yield more benefits to employers than shorter programmes, and that most apprenticeships can be offered with a high apprentice wage, while being still profitable for firms. Similarly, Wolter and Joho (2018[32]) used data from Switzerland to simulate the costs and benefits of apprenticeships and rates of return to individuals in the English context considering different scenarios. The analysis suggested, for example, that programmes that last at least three years and engage young apprentices have the most favourable cost-benefit balance for firms.

Conclusion

This chapter asks whether apprenticeships can provide a useful contribution to every country, and finds that across the OECD, apprenticeships are training learners in an ever-growing range of occupations. They are no longer the preserve of the trades and crafts, nor of the private sector. The distinct advantages of apprenticeships as a learning approach are universal: the heavy engagement of employers signalling the clear labour market demand for skills being developed, and work-based learning ensuring that the technical and soft skills developed are highly relevant to actual workplaces. However, specific national (or regional) circumstances are likely to make them more or less attractive, and the particular circumstances of countries, sectors and occupations create predictable challenges that policy must address.

High-quality apprenticeship provision balances the needs of the employer, sector and apprentice (as commonly delivered through social partnership) and ensures that no artificial barriers make apprenticeships less attractive than alternative learning pathways. Countries introducing apprenticeships should be aware that they are easier to implement where formal qualifications bring clear benefits to learners, as in the licenced occupations.

There are many ways of organising apprenticeships. One size does not fit all. The challenge is to identify the approaches that work for both employers and learners. It should be expected that the design features of apprenticeships (e.g. choices concerning wages, duration and funding) will vary by national and sectoral context to ensure that apprenticeships are attractive to both employers and prospective apprentices. There are now established methodologies which enable governments to analyse the costs and benefits of apprenticeships. Survey tools can provide empirical evidence to help policy makers get the balance right.

Note

[1] Called traineeships.

References

Acemoglu, D. and J. Pischke (1999), "Beyond becker: Training in imperfect labour markets", *The Economic Journal*, Vol. 109/453, pp. 112-142, http://dx.doi.org/10.1111/1468-0297.00405. [28]

BIBB (2018), *Inter-company Vocational Training Centres*, http://www.bibb.de/en/12303.php (accessed on 3 April 2018). [16]

BIBB (2017), *2017 Ranglisten*, (Ranking 2017), Federal Institute for Vocational Training, Bonn, https://www.bibb.de/dokumente/pdf/a21_naa309_2017_PM_Ranglisten_20180307.pdf. [6]

Blanchard, O. and A. Landier (2002), "The perverse effects of partial labour market reform: Fixed-term contracts in France", *The Economic Journal*, Vol. 112/480, pp. F214-F244, http://www.jstor.org/stable/798373. [22]

Breen, R. (2005), "Explaining cross-national variation in youth unemployment: Market and institutional factors on JSTOR", *European Sociological Review*, Vol. 21/2, pp. 125-134, http://www.jstor.org/stable/3559487. [24]

Condon, N. and J. Mcnaboe (2016), *Monitoring Ireland's Skills Supply. Trends in Education and Training Outputs*, SOLAS, Dublin, http://www.solas.ie/SolasPdfLibrary/Monitoring%20Ireland's%20Skills%20Supply%20Report%202016.pdf. [12]

De Rick, K. (2008), "Costs and benefits of apprenticeships in the lowest track of VET", in Schlögl, P. (ed.), *Situated Competence Development through Innovative Apprenticeships. The Role Of Different Stakeholders, Conference Proceedings* , Österreichisches Institut für Berufsbildungsforschung, Vienna. [25]

Dionisius, R. et al. (2008), "Cost and benefit of apprenticeship training: A comparison of Germany and Switzerland", *Discussion Paper Series*, No. 3465, IZA, Bonn, http://ftp.iza.org/dp3465.pdf. [30]

DOL (2018), *United States Department of Labor, Training and Employment Notice 3-18*, https://wdr.doleta.gov/directives/corr_doc.cfm?docn=5367. [3]

EUR-Lex (2018), *Council Recommendation of 15 March 2018 on a European Framework for Quality and Effective Apprenticeships*, https://eur-lex.europa.eu/legal-content/EN/TXT/?uri=CELEX:32018H0502(01). [20]

FDEA (2008), *National Report from Switzerland Contributing to the OECD Learning for Jobs Review*, Swiss Confederation Federal Department of Economic Affairs. [17]

Federal Statistics Office (FSO) (2018), *Vocational Education and Training (VET) – Schools*, http://www.bfs.admin.ch/bfs/en/home/statistics/education-science/pupils-students/upper-secondary/vocational-training.html (accessed on 1 July 2018). [5]

GOV.UK (2016), *Civil Service Fast Track Apprenticeship Schemes*, http://www.gov.uk/guidance/civil-service-fast-track-apprenticeship-fast-track-schemes (accessed on 1 July 2018). [8]

Hargreaves, J., J. Stanwick and P. Skujins (2017), *The Changing Nature of Apprenticeships: 1996-2016*, National Centre for Vocational Education Research, Adelaide, https://www.ncver.edu.au/publications/publications/all-publications/the-changing-nature-of-apprenticeships-1996-2016. [10]

Hoeckel, K., S. Field and W. Grubb (2009), *OECD Reviews of Vocational Education and Training: A Learning for Jobs Review of Switzerland 2009*, OECD Publishing, Paris, http://dx.doi.org/10.1787/9789264113985-en. [15]

Kahn, L. (2016), "Permanent jobs, employment protection and job content", *IZA Discussion Paper Series*, No. 9961, Institute for the Study of Labor (IZA), Bonn, http://ftp.iza.org/dp9961.pdf. [23]

Koumenta, M. et al. (2014), *Occupational Regulation in the EU and UK: Prevalence and Labour Market Impacts*, Queen Mary University of London, London, https://www.gov.uk/government/uploads/system/uploads/attachment_data/file/343554/bis-14-999-occupational-regulation-in-the-EU-and-UK.pdf. [21]

Kuczera, M. (2017), "Striking the right balance: Costs and benefits of apprenticeship", *OECD Education Working Papers*, No. 153, OECD Publishing, Paris, http://dx.doi.org/10.1787/995fff01-en. [2]

Kuczera, M., T. Bastianić and S. Field (2018), *Apprenticeship and Vocational Education and Training in Israel*, OECD Reviews of Vocational Education and Training, OECD Publishing, Paris, https://doi.org/10.1787/9789264302051-en. [19]

Kuczera, M. et al. (2008), *OECD Reviews of Vocational Education and Training: A Learning for Jobs Review of Norway 2008*, OECD Publishing, Paris, http://dx.doi.org/10.1787/9789264113947-en. [14]

Kuczera, M. and S. Field (2018), *Apprenticeship in England, United Kingdom*, OECD Reviews of Vocational Education and Training, OECD Publishing, Paris, http://dx.doi.org/10.1787/9789264298507-en. [13]

Lanning, T. (2011), "Why rethink apprenticeships?", in Dolphin, T. and T. Lanning (eds.), *Rethinking Apprenticeships*, Institute for Public Policy Research, London, https://www.ippr.org/files/images/media/files/publication/2011/11/apprenticeships_Nov2011_8028.pdf. [11]

Moretti, L. et al. (2017), "So similar and yet so different: A comparative analysis of a firm's cost and benefits of apprenticeship training in Austria and Switzerland", *IZA Discussion Paper Series*, No. 11081, IZA - Institute of Labor Economics, Bonn, http://ftp.iza.org/dp11081.pdf. [18]

Mühlemann, S. (2016), "The cost and benefits of work-based learning", *OECD Education Working Papers*, No. 143, OECD Publishing, Paris, https://doi.org/10.1787/5jlpl4s6g0zv-en. [29]

Mühlemann, S. and M. Leiser (2015), "Ten facts you need to know about hiring", *IZA Discussion Paper Series*, No. 9363, IZA - Institute for the Study of Labor , Bonn, http://ftp.iza.org/dp9363.pdf. [27]

OECD (2017), *OECD Employment Outlook 2017*, OECD Publishing, Paris, http://dx.doi.org/10.1787/empl_outlook-2017-en. [4]

OECD (2010), *Learning for Jobs*, OECD Reviews of Vocational Education and Training, OECD Publishing, Paris, https://doi.org/10.1787/9789264087460-en. [1]

Strupler, M., S. Wolter and M. Moser (2012), *Die duale Lehre : eine Erfolgsgeschichte - auch für die Betriebe : Ergebnisse der dritten Kosten-Nutzen-Erhebung der Lehrlingsausbildung aus der Sicht der Betriebe*, (Dual training: A Success Story for Companies: Results of the 3rd Cost-benefit Survey in the Eyes of Entreprises), Rüegger. [26]

Watson, D., S. McCoy and S. Gorby (2006), "The post-leaving certificate sector in Ireland: A multivariate analysis of educational and employment outcomes", *Research Series*, No. BMI189, Economic and Social Research Institute (ESRI), https://ideas.repec.org/b/esr/resser/bmi189.html. [9]

Wirtschaftskammer Österreich (WKO) (2018), *Hauptergebnisse der WKO - Lehrlingstatistik*, (Main Results of the Trainee Statistics of the Austrian Economic Chambers), Austrian Economic Chambers, Wien, https://www.wko.at/service/zahlen-daten-fakten/daten-lehrlingsstatistik.html (accessed on 19 April 2018). [7]

Wolter, S. and E. Joho (2018), *Apprenticeship Training in England – A Cost-effective Model for Firms?*, Education Policy Institute, Bertelsmann Stiftung and JP Morgan Chase Foundation, https://www.bertelsmann-stiftung.de/fileadmin/files/BSt/Publikationen/GrauePublikationen/LL_cost_benefit_study_England.pdf. [32]

Wolter, S. and S. Mühlemann (2015), *Apprenticeship Training in Spain: A Cost-effective Model for Firms?*, Bertelsmann Stiftung, Gütersloh, https://www.bertelsmann-stiftung.de/en/publications/publication/did/apprecenticeship-training-in-spain-a-cost-effective-model-for-firms/. [31]

Chapter 2. Should employers receive financial incentives to provide apprenticeships?

This chapter considers the issue of employer-focused financial incentives within apprenticeship policy. It explores the public interest in apprenticeship provision and describes how countries make funding available to employers through tax incentives, subsidies and levy systems. The chapter describes the challenges and risks associated with financial incentives, before exploring other means by which governments can make apprenticeships more attractive to employers, including mechanisms designed to improve in-company training and to reduce administrative costs. The chapter ends with a consideration of the additional apprenticeship costs typically encountered by small employers.

Issues and challenges

Encouraging apprenticeship provision is a challenge in many countries

Many countries have been grappling with the challenge of getting employers on board to support apprenticeships. Employer support is often the key challenge in either improving or expanding existing schemes, or building new apprenticeship schemes from scratch. A key question is how much public support should be given to apprenticeships and what form it should take to effectively encourage employers to take on apprentices.

The benefits of apprenticeships to society underpin the rationale for public support

When companies offer high-quality youth apprenticeships, they shoulder the burden of training and guiding young people through to employment. The skills developed involve a mix of firm and occupation-specific skills, as well as generic skills (e.g. teamwork, literacy, numeracy), which will carry individual workers through their careers and help them adapt to changing requirements. However, some of the benefits will also be more widely shared, impacting on the state and society in the form of higher employment rates and productivity, better health, lower reliance on welfare measures and reduced criminality rates. One study from the United States estimates that over the career of an apprentice, social benefits outweigh the social costs by over USD 49 000 (Reed et al., 2012[1]). These wider benefits to the state and society strengthen the rationale for public financial support for apprenticeships.

For the state, apprenticeships tend to cost less than school-based options

From the perspective of public spending, apprenticeships are a cost-effective way of developing workplace skills. The alternative often involves teaching practical skills in school workshops, where specialised equipment and teaching staff are costly. Even taking into account the cost of government subsidies, the cost of apprenticeships to the state can be less than that of school-based vocational education and training (VET) (Westergaard-Nielsen and Rasmussen, 1999[2]). In addition, apprenticeships yield wider benefits that are hard to realise for school-based programmes (e.g. connecting apprentices to employers, allowing learning on the latest equipment) (OECD, 2010[3]).

One form of support is state-funded school-based learning for youth apprenticeships

In countries where apprenticeships mainly serve young people, they form one of the routes to an upper-secondary qualification, alongside general or school-based vocational programmes. If school-based pathways receive state funding, public support for apprenticeships is partly a matter of fairness. Across OECD countries, the school-based component of apprenticeships at the upper-secondary level is typically funded by the state and offered free of charge to apprentices. The issue is somewhat different in countries where most apprentices are adults (e.g. Canada and the United States), and where apprenticeships are an alternative to employee training or a route to a post-secondary qualification.

It is fair to expect employers to bear some of the costs of apprenticeship provision?

Given that the benefits from apprenticeships are shared with employers and more widely, governments should not be expected to cover all the costs involved. Employers should also contribute as they reap benefits when taking on apprentices (see Muehlemann (2016[4]) for a review of the literature). Some benefits to employers are realised when apprentices contribute to productive work while in the company. Initially, untrained apprentices contribute little, and they tend to earn very low wages, but more experienced apprentices have productivity levels closer to that of a skilled employee, and they still cost less than skilled workers (see Chapter 3 for more on apprentice wages). In addition, once the apprenticeship is completed there is another opportunity to benefit: companies can save money on recruitment by selecting and recruiting as employees the strongest apprentices at the end of training, rather than hiring from the external labour market (this is further discussed below).

The key question is how best to support apprenticeships with public resources

Beyond supporting apprenticeships through the school-based component, governments sometimes offer incentives to promote apprenticeships in two broad forms:

- Financial incentives: direct subsidies or tax breaks (Table 2.1 provides an overview of financial incentives used in selected OECD countries).
- Non-financial incentives: measures designed to reduce the costs of offering apprenticeships or increase the benefits without financial transfers.

Information and evidence on such incentives and their effectiveness is set out in Table 2.1.

Table 2.1. Financial incentives designed to encourage employers to offer apprenticeships

	Tax incentives	Subsidy	Levy scheme
Australia	No	Yes, a range of payments are made to eligible employers under the Australian Apprenticeships Incentives Program.	No
Austria	Abolished in 2008 and replaced by subsidies	Yes, per apprentice (amount depends on the year of training) and for additional training, supervisor training, apprentices who excel in final assessments, measures for apprentices with learning difficulties, and measures for equal access of men and women.	A levy fund in the construction sector covering all regions and in the electro-metallic industry in one province (Vorarlberg). Negotiated by the employers and trade union.
Flanders (Belgium)	Payroll tax deduction	Yes, depending on the number of apprentices and programme duration, including bonuses for the mentor and apprentice.	No
Denmark	No	No	All firms pay a contribution to the Employer Reimbursement Fund (AER) based on the number of full-time employees. Firms with apprentices get their expenses refunded when apprentices are at VET college. AER also pays grants to encourage the provision of additional training places.
England (United Kingdom)	No	Contributions from employers who pay the levy are topped up with a 10% contribution from the government. Grants to firms and education and training institutions offering apprenticeships to 16-18 year-olds.	Universal levy set at 0.5% of payroll, applying to the proportion of payroll above GBP 3 million.
Germany	No	No	In the building sector. Negotiated by employers and trade unions.
Netherlands	Abolished in 2014	Yes, to employers providing apprenticeships (maximum EUR 2 700 per student per year), depending on the duration of the apprenticeship and the number of training companies asking for subsidies.	No
Norway	No	Yes, per apprentice depending on apprentice characteristics (e.g. age, disability, school performance, migration status, gender, previous education) and sector characteristics.	No
Switzerland	No	No	All companies within some economic sectors are required to contribute to a corresponding vocational and professional education and training (VPET) fund. The Confederation may declare some VPET funds to be of general interest and therefore mandatory for all companies within a given economic sector.

Note: Tax incentives reduce either the tax base or the tax due. They include: 1) tax allowances (deducted from the gross income to arrive at the taxable income); 2) tax exemptions (some particular income is exempted from the tax base); 3) tax credits (sums deducted from the tax due); 4) tax relief (some classes of taxpayers or activities benefit from lower rates); and 5) tax deferrals (postponement of tax payments).
Source: Kuczera, M. (2017[5]), "Striking the right balance: Costs and benefits of apprenticeship", *OECD Education Working Papers*, No. 153, http://dx.doi.org/10.1787/995fff01-en.

Financial incentives to encourage employers to take on apprentices should be used with caution

There is a strong argument for governments to dedicate public resources to support apprenticeships, given the role of apprenticeships in preparing individuals for a job and a career, and the wider social benefits that apprenticeships yield. Many countries face the challenge of securing enough apprenticeship placements in firms. As a result, financial incentives have been widely used to encourage employers to offer more placements. Whether the use of financial incentives is desirable depends partly on the targeted policy objective.

Financial incentives may be offered to reward firms that recruit apprentices in recognition of the fact that by doing so they shoulder a burden that would otherwise be carried by the state: the task of preparing young people for a career. This rationale may underpin incentives offered to all firms that take apprentices, regardless of the impact of the incentives on the provision of apprenticeship places.

However, international experience suggests that financial incentives should be used with caution and carefully evaluated.

- Universal incentives give all firms that take apprentices a fixed sum, and have a small impact on firms' provision of apprenticeship places.
- Targeted incentives are designed to focus resources on placements that would not be offered in the absence of incentives. They may reward firms that take apprentices with certain characteristics (e.g. disadvantaged youth, disabled people) or be available only to certain sectors or types of firms (e.g. small firms). In theory such incentives may have more impact, but they are costlier to implement and their effectiveness will depend on how precisely the scheme is designed. When targeted incentives are used, their impact should be carefully evaluated and compared to alternative tools (e.g. supporting training capacity in firms).
- Employers may have an interest in setting up a levy to share the costs of training between firms when the labour market is tight and it is hard to find skilled employees on the external labour market, and when employers face a high risk that their fully trained apprentices will be poached by other firms. Money collected through a levy may then be used to offer incentives to employers that take on apprentices.

Policy argument 1: Universal incentives are likely to have little impact

Financial incentives make a difference only at the margins

A universal incentive scheme offering all firms a fixed sum for taking on an apprentice has its appeal – for government it is cheaper to administer, for employers it is easier to understand. However, such schemes are bound to have limited overall impact because a small incentive spread across many apprenticeships will only change the behaviour of the small minority of employers who can be coaxed into taking an apprentice, or more apprentices, by a small financial reward.

The balance at the end of an apprenticeship varies across firms and occupations

One reason for the small impact of a general subsidy is that the net benefits of apprenticeships to employers are very variable. Financial incentives will make a difference only for firms that initially found apprenticeships not worthwhile and for whom the extra money changed the balance from negative to break even or slightly positive, which is likely to be a relatively small share of employers. Net benefits to employers from apprenticeships vary a lot according to occupation (Figure 2.1 shows data from Switzerland), and firm size (Mühlemann, 2016[4]). The nature of the occupation matters: apprentice gardeners can make themselves useful at work quickly, but would-be electronics technicians need substantial training with expensive equipment before being productive.

Figure 2.1. In Switzerland, the net benefits of apprenticeship to employers vary widely between different occupations

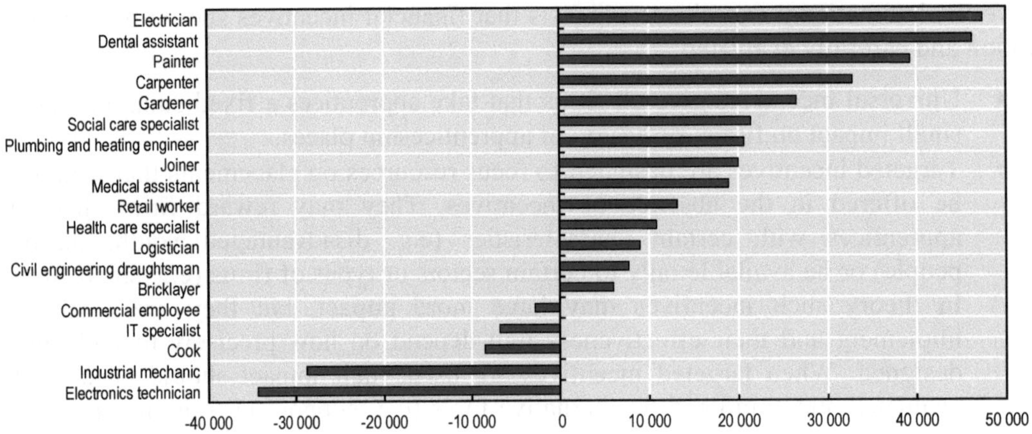

Note: Reference year 2009.
Source: Mühlemann, S (2016[4]), "The cost and benefits of work-based learning", *OECD Education Working Papers*, No. 143, https://doi.org/10.1787/5jlpl4s6g0zv-en.

StatLink http://dx.doi.org/10.1787/888933828391

International evidence offers limited support for universal financial incentives

In Denmark, subsidies have only had an impact in some sectors: manufacturing, office and retail (Westergaard-Nielsen and Rasmussen, 1999[2]). In Australia and Austria, subsidies seem to have only had a small impact on apprenticeship provision by employers (Wacker, 2007[6]; Deloitte Access Economics, 2012[7]). Research based on Swiss data suggests that costs influence a firm's decision to train, but once a firm has decided to train these costs have little impact on the number of apprentices it takes on. To have a significant impact, the subsidy should concentrate efforts on firms that do not train and exclude those that already have apprentices – while this may be attractive on theoretical grounds and has been tried in some countries, it might be seen as unfair and unfeasible from a political and practical point of view (Mühlemann et al., 2007[8]).

Policy argument 2: Targeted incentives may have more impact, but they are hard to implement

Targeting financial incentives where they make a difference is appealing in theory

In the economist's ideal world, the money would only go to those companies where extra money shifts the net benefits of apprenticeships from negative to break even or slightly positive. The amount of the incentive would be set at a level that just makes the difference, so that employers change their minds and hire another apprentice – one euro more would be a gift from the public purse to the firm, one euro less would fail to make a difference.

But effective targeting is difficult

Identifying apprenticeship placements that would not have been offered without the extra money is a challenge. Some schemes focus on additionality. For example, Germany introduced a scheme in 2008 that targeted young people who failed to find an apprenticeship, but it was scrapped two years later due to a lack of impact (Bonin, 2013[9]). Additionality tests can be hard to enforce given the churn of turnover. It may also be seen as unfair if funding does not go to employers with a stable and long-standing commitment to apprenticeships. Other schemes focus on apprentices or occupations where policy makers expect fewer available apprenticeship placements in the absence of support. In Austria, Australia and Norway, employers taking on disadvantaged apprentices qualify for extra subsidies. France allows a higher tax break for such firms (see Chapter 6). Sometimes specific occupations are targeted, such as shortage occupations in Australia, or small crafts in Norway (Kuczera, 2017[10]).

Targeted incentives risk moving training efforts from one group to another

Offering financial incentives to target a specific group may increase one type of training at the expense of others. Such effects are sometimes intended, since funding criteria are designed to set priorities. However, sometimes there are unwanted effects. For example, in the Netherlands, a 1998 tax law sought to encourage the training of older workers through a higher tax break if training was offered to workers over 40. Research found that the overall training volume barely changed and that training was redistributed from workers slightly below the age of 40 to those just over 40 (Leuven and Oosterbeek, 2004[11]).

Policy argument 3: Sectoral levies may support training in some sectors

Levies are a special case, with money coming from employers

Training levies typically collect money for financial incentives from employers instead of all taxpayers. The costs of levy-funded financial incentives fall on employers collectively, making some employers winners and others losers. The winners are those who pay little into the scheme but take advantage of it, for example by having many apprentices supported by levy funding. The aim of levy schemes is to reward employers that offer apprenticeships and make those who benefit indirectly (by poaching skilled workers trained by other firms) contribute to the cost of training. The overall amount of training should increase towards a more optimal and socially efficient level since the measure corrects for the market failure involved in this free riding. Some effects are not strictly economic. Levy schemes that require employers to be directly involved in managing the fund and identifying priorities are commonly intended to give employers a stronger sense of involvement and ownership in the training.

Sectoral levies tend to have stronger employer support

Few countries have levy systems specifically designed to support apprenticeships. In Denmark and France, all employers share the cost of apprenticeships. Recent reforms to introduce a national levy for larger employers to support apprenticeships in England (United Kingdom) are being watched with interest. Often not all employers contribute to levies. Sectoral levies are established when employers in the same sector see apprenticeships as being in their collective interest. In this case, they may opt to work together to support training through a levy. Employer commitment to sectoral levies is usually high, and such schemes exist in many European countries. Employers have strong incentives to set up such a levy when apprenticeship training is costly, the labour market is tight and it is hard to find skilled recruits on the external labour market, and when firms face a high risk of their employees being poached by others. Employers tend to be more sceptical of universal levy schemes, which they often perceive as a tax, and where companies have little control over how the money is used (Müller and Behringer, 2012[12]).

Box 2.1. Sectoral training levies in Switzerland

Professional organisations can request that the Federal Council sets up a mandatory sectoral fund, with all companies in the sector paying solidarity contributions for the provision of VET (e.g. development of regulations, pedagogical and teaching materials). The amount of contribution depends on the company payroll. Currently, nearly 30 funds are in place. Companies reported that the role of the fund was to increase solidarity in sharing the cost of VET. An evaluation showed that the setting up of such funds is easier in well-organised sectors/industries, that the administrative cost of contributing to the fund incurred by the company should be as low as possible, and that the use of funds should be transparent. The impact of funds on apprenticeship provision and its outcomes has not yet been evaluated.

Source: SEFRI (2009[13]), *Évaluation Des Fonds En Faveur de La Formation Professionnelle*, Secrétariat d'Etat à la formation, à la recherche et à l'innovation, Confédération suisse, www.sbfi.admin.ch/sbfi/fr/home/bildung/berufsbildungssteuerung-und--politik/berufsbildungsfinanzierung/fonds-en-faveur-de-la-formation-professionnelle-selon-art--60-lf/evaluation-des-fonds-en-faveur-de-la-formation-professionnelle.html; SEFRI (2017[14]), *Fonds En Faveur de La Formation Professionnelle Entrés En Vigueur Selon l'art. 60 LFPr*, Secrétariat d'Etat à la formation, à la recherche et à l'innovation, www.sbfi.admin.ch/sbfi/fr/home/bildung/berufsbildungssteuerung-und--politik/berufsbildungsfinanzierung/fonds-en-faveur-de-la-formation-professionnelle-selon-art--60-lf.html.

Policy argument 4: Financial incentives may have undesirable side effects

Large companies are better placed to benefit from financial support

Another challenge associated with financial incentives is that they tend to benefit large employers disproportionately (Müller and Behringer, 2012[12]). To benefit from financial incentives, employers need to be informed about available schemes (e.g. criteria of eligibility and application procedure), build training plans accordingly and file applications and follow-up with documentation as required. This is often easier for bigger employers with dedicated departments and training staff, especially if they go through the same procedure for several apprentices. This means that small firms may struggle to access available funding opportunities. When financial incentives are offered, it is therefore important to assist small firms with access to funding.

Regulations need to ensure that financial incentives are not used to sustain low-quality apprenticeships

Financial incentives – particularly large incentives - can sometimes encourage firms to offer apprenticeships for the wrong reasons. Apprenticeships involve costs, for which employers can make up by ensuring apprentices become highly productive, contributing to production and sometimes staying on as an employee after completion. This requires commitment to quality on-the-job training. With subsidies in the picture, apprenticeships may become financially appealing to employers even if they offer little training. This seems to have happened in Australia, where the withdrawal of a subsidy led to a fall in apprenticeship placements in some sectors, such as services (Pfeifer, 2016[15]). In the affected sectors employers rarely hired apprentices upon completion and poor employment outcomes were pointing to quality problems (Mühlemann, 2016[4]).

To encourage employers, governments should aim to improve the apprenticeship cost-benefit balance through system design, support and capacity building

Attention should focus on non-financial incentives that improve the cost-benefit balance to employers, such as readjusting the design of apprenticeship schemes and enhancing training capacity in companies. Governments and social partners can support smaller employers by:

- Encouraging employers to find ways to share the responsibilities and risks associated with the provision of apprenticeships.
- Promoting bodies that work with groups of small employers to co-ordinate training.
- Supporting small employers with the administration and provision of apprenticeships.

International evidence offers limited support for the use of financial incentives, but there are many other ways of making apprenticeships appealing to employers. Design features of apprenticeship schemes can be adjusted so that they work better for employers (as set out in Chapter 1), and these can be augmented by capacity-building measures, which aim to support employers and get the best out of apprentices.

Policy argument 1: Supporting employers that offer apprenticeships can help them achieve a more favourable cost-benefit balance

Apprenticeships can be promoted by making firms better at training

One way of helping employers achieve a better return from apprenticeships is to help them improve their in-company training. Better training yields higher benefits for the firm: through careful management, apprentices can be better integrated into the production process, they develop skills faster and contribute to production with their skills earlier. Training capacity within a firm depends on the quality of trainers, as well as the training methods and equipment used. Measures to improve training capacity may have a particularly large impact on small firms that lack dedicated training staff, and make it easier for them to offer apprenticeships. Policy measures that develop training capacity in firms are further discussed in Chapter 5.

External bodies may also offer further support to employers

Several countries have established external bodies that take over some of the tasks generated by the provision of apprenticeships. This may include the search for a suitable apprentice, or dealing with administrative tasks. In some countries, such bodies even sign the contract with the apprentice and hire out apprentices to employers for training. Such arrangements can make it easier and cheaper for employers to offer apprenticeships. Some aim to match firms to individuals looking for an apprenticeship position. Depending on the country, these bodies are run and managed by employers themselves, or by a third party.

Box 2.2. External bodies supporting apprenticeship training

Australia

Group training organisations (GTOs) are predominantly not-for-profit organisations supported by public authorities, with some charges to host employers. GTOs employ apprentices and hire them out to host employers, sometimes focusing on a particular industry or region. Their tasks include: selecting apprentices adapted to the needs of employers; arranging and monitoring training both on and-off-the job; taking care of administrative duties; and ensuring that apprentices receive a broad range of training experience, sometimes by rotating them to different firms.

Source: OECD (2010[31]), *Learning for Jobs*, OECD Reviews of Vocational Education and Training, https://doi.org/10.1787/9789264087460-en.

Norway

Training offices (*opplæringskontor*) are owned by companies and funded through state grants (firms typically pay half of the apprenticeship subsidy they receive to training agencies). They aim to establish new apprenticeship places, supervise training firms, train apprentice supervisors and deal with administrative tasks. Many training offices organise the theoretical part of training and sign the apprenticeship contracts on behalf of firms. About 70-80% of firms with apprentices are associated with training offices. Research shows that training offices played an important role in supporting apprenticeships and ensuring their quality.

Source: Høst, H. (2015[16]), *Kvalitet i fag- og yrkesopplæringen, Sluttrapport, Fafo-rapport 2015:32*, www.fafo.no/index.php/zoo-publikasjoner/fafo-rapporter/item/kvalitet-i-fag-og-yrkesopplaeringen-sluttrapport-2; Høst, H., A. Skålholt and A. Nyen, (2012[17]), *The OECD International Survey of VET Systems, 2007 – Norway* (unpublished).

Regulatory measures can encourage apprenticeship provision

The simplest type of regulatory measure is a workforce requirement. For example, a new requirement in England (United Kingdom) is that larger (more than 250 employees) public sector providers should have at least 2.3% of their workforce as apprentices. Companies providing apprenticeships can be rewarded with preferential treatment in the award of public contracts. The evaluation of this policy in Switzerland (Leiser and Wolter, 2017[18]) found that it increased apprenticeship provision among small firms and in sectors where public procurement represents a large share of the business, while maintaining training quality. While preferential treatment in the award of public contracts looks promising given its relatively low cost and the positive impact, there are some potential drawbacks: 1) some highly specialised firms have niche skilled jobs that will not correspond to any widely recognised apprentice qualification, and they may be discriminated against in the public procurement process; 2) there may be discrimination against small firms when a limited pool of qualified applicants for apprenticeships are scooped up by larger firms; and 3) the policy may lead to too many apprenticeships in certain industries or occupations (such as construction) where public procurement is widespread (Mühlemann, 2016[4]; Leiser and Wolter, 2017[18]).

Policy argument 2: Small employers require special attention

Small employers face particular barriers

Many countries are concerned that smaller employers may be reluctant to offer apprenticeships, and it has been argued that funds from training levies are often exploited by larger employers (Johanson, 2009[19]; Dar and Whitehead, 2003[20]; Cedefop, 2011[21]; Müller and Behringer, 2012[12]). Some smaller employers may lack the capacity to plan and determine training needs, and they will be less efficient in offering training. Large firms, however, can train several apprentices using one instructor and it is easier for them to bear the fixed costs of dealing with administrative requirements. Small firms may also be unable to train for the full range of skills required by a particular apprenticeship qualification. International evidence suggests that small firms are indeed less likely than large firms to offer apprenticeships. In Switzerland, participation in training greatly increases with size of enterprise (Bliem, Petanovitsch and Schmid, 2016[22]). Whereas around 25% of companies with fewer than 10 employees provide apprenticeships, it is 80% of large firms employing 100 people or more (Mühlemann, 2016[4]). Simulations for apprenticeships in England (United Kingdom) found that firms with fewer than 10 employees struggle to reap net benefits, so in sectors where the role of apprentices is crucial, targeted measures may be needed to encourage their engagement (Wolter and Joho, 2018[23]).

Small employers rely on the prospect of long-term benefits less than large ones

In the short-term balance (i.e. during apprenticeships), large firms do not achieve better results than small firms. This is because while large firms may be more efficient in offering training, this is counterbalanced by their tendency to train more in costly technical fields (Mühlemann, 2016[4]). The difference in terms of expected benefits lies in the longer term: the scope for reaping benefits by retaining apprentices upon completion is less for smaller firms. One reason is that the bigger the firm, the more likely it is to retain apprenticeship graduates as skilled workers (see Figure 2.2 for data from Germany and Switzerland). This may be because small firms cannot offer a job to their qualified apprentice as a skilled worker, or because their apprenticeship graduates prefer to work for larger employers with better career prospects. Even when small employers retain apprentices as skilled employees, the savings realised by the recruitment will be smaller because these savings depend on the cost of the alternative option (i.e. hiring an external recruit), and hiring costs tend to be smaller in smaller firms. This is partly driven by the nature of the jobs offered: larger firms are more likely to operate in technical sectors where new recruits need costly training at the start, so hiring costs are higher. Also, small firms often train only one apprentice at a time, so it would be risky to rely on the prospect of recruitment to make up for the costs involved. For example, if after three or four years of training the apprentice decides to take up a job offer elsewhere, it would take the firm another three or four years to fill a vacancy (Mühlemann, 2016[4]). A larger firm that trains several apprentices takes less of a risk – if one apprentice opts for a job elsewhere, they can still hire one of the remaining apprentices. The implication is that in the absence of long-term benefits from recruitment, many small firms will only provide apprenticeships if they can recoup their investment by the end of the training period.

Figure 2.2. Company retention rates of apprentices (by number of employees)

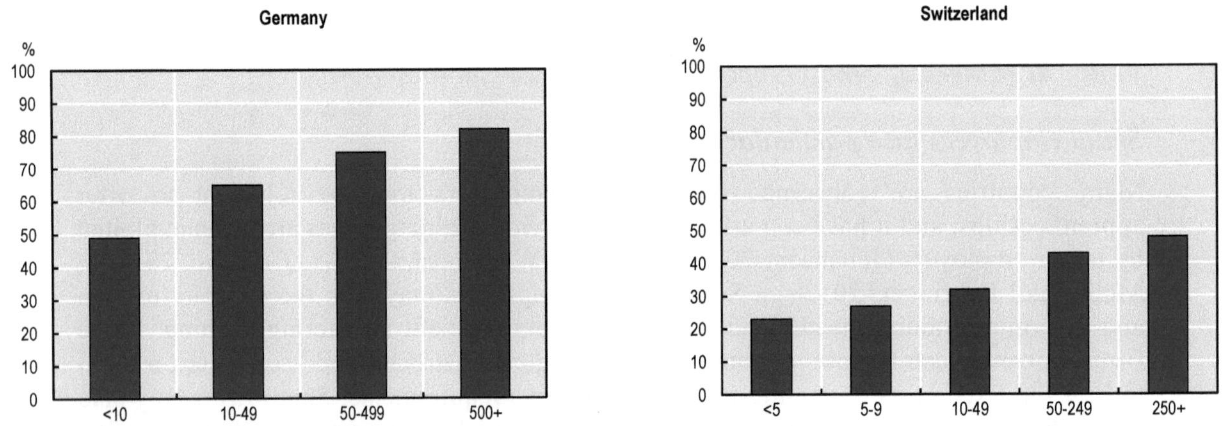

Note: 2012/13 for Germany and 2009 for Switzerland.
Source: Adapted from Mühlemann, S. (2016[4]), "The cost and benefits of work-based learning", *OECD Education Working Papers*, No. 143, https://doi.org/10.1787/5jlpl4s6g0zv-en.

StatLink http://dx.doi.org/10.1787/888933828410

Small employers can play a major role in providing apprenticeships

Despite these hurdles, across OECD countries small employers are major providers of apprenticeships. In countries with available data from the Survey of Adult Skills, a product of the Programme for the International Assessment of Adult Competencies (PIAAC) (i.e. Austria, Australia, Canada, Denmark, the Netherlands), over half of all apprentices work in firms with 50 or fewer employees (Kuczera, 2017[10]). In Germany, 39% of apprentices work in firms with fewer than 50 employees (BIBB, 2017[24]).

This reflects both the large share of small firms in OECD economies and the fact that when small firms train apprentices, they tend to do it in a more "intensive" way than larger firms. In some countries with large apprenticeship systems, the ratio of apprentices to total employees (training ratio) among firms that offer apprenticeships is larger in small firms and decreases with firm size. In Switzerland, the ratio of apprentices to total employees (the training ratio) was between 7.5% and 9% in training companies with fewer than 10 employees, 4% in training companies with 50-99 employees, and 3% in training companies with over 1 000 employees. In Austria, the training ratio was 5% in training companies with fewer than 50 employees but just under 4% for training companies with more than 50 employees (Bliem, Petanovitsch and Schmid, 2016[22]).

Conclusion

This chapter questions whether employers should receive financial incentives to provide apprenticeships and argues that there is a case for public funding to support apprenticeships. It is fair that young people can expect comparable levels of support as they are prepared for working life, and the strong employment outcomes linked to apprenticeships lead to net savings for the state. Governments should consider incentives such as tax breaks and subsidies for employers, however, only with great caution as risks are high that funding will fail to drive the behaviour intended. One exception relates to employer levies, particularly in specific sectors, which can be designed to accentuate employer ownership over training. Governments are better served by targeting funding at measures that will increase the speed with which apprentices develop skills and so become productive. Such measures include help to improve the quality of in-company training and the reduction of administrative costs related to apprenticeships. Costs are structurally higher for smaller employers of apprentices and warrant special attention.

References

BIBB (2017), *Datenreport zum Berufsbildungsbericht 2017*, (Data Report for the Report on Vocational Education and Training for the Year 2017), Federal Institute for Vocational Training, Bonn, http://www.bibb.de/dokumente/pdf/bibb_datenreport_2017.pdf. [24]

Bliem, W., A. Petanovitsch and K. Schmid (2016), *Dual Vocational Education and Training in Austria, Germany, Liechtenstein and Switzerland*, Institut für Bildungsforschung der Wirtschaft, Vienna, http://www.dcdualvet.org/wp-content/uploads/Dual-VET-Comparative-Study_Full-Study.pdf. [22]

Bonin, H. (2013), *Begleitforschung "Auswirkungen des Ausbildungsbonus auf den Ausbildungsmarkt und die öffentlichen Haushalte"*, (Accompanying Research. Impacts of the Training Bonus on the Training Market and Public Budgets), Bundesministerium fürArbeit und Soziales, Berlin, http://www.bmas.de/SharedDocs/Downloads/DE/PDF-Publikationen/Forschungsberichte/fb438-Ausbildungsbonus-2013.pdf?__blob=publicationFile. [9]

Cedefop (2011), *Using Tax Incentives to Promote Education and Training: Cedefop Panorama Series 2009*, Office for Official Publications of the European Communities, Luxembourg, http://www.cedefop.europa.eu/fr/publications-and-resources/publications/5180. [21]

Dar, A. and T. Whitehead (2003), *Training Levies: Evidence from Evaluations*, The World Bank, Washington DC, http://documents.worldbank.org/curated/en/705121468779070378/Training-levies-evidence-from-evaluations. [20]

Deloitte Access Economics (2012), *Econometric Analysis of the Australian Apprenticeships Incentives Program*, Deloitte Access Economics, Barton, https://www.australianapprenticeships.gov.au/sites/ausapps/files/publication-documents/econometricanalysisaaip.pdf. [7]

Høst, H. (2015), *Kvalitet i fag- og yrkesopplæringen. Sluttrapport | Fafo-rapport 2015:32*, (Quality in Vocational Education and Training. Final Report), NIFU (Nordic Institute for the Study of Innovation, Research and Education), Oslo, http://www.fafo.no/index.php/zoo-publikasjoner/fafo-rapporter/item/kvalitet-i-fag-og-yrkesopplaeringen-sluttrapport-2. [16]

Høst, H., A. Skålholt and A. Nyen (2012), *Om potensialet for å få bedriftene til å ta inn flere lærlinger: En kartlegging av norske bedrifters vurdering av lærlingordningen*, (The Potential of Having Companies Accepting More Apprentices: A Review of How Norwegian Companies Assess the Apprenticeship Scheme), NIFU (Nordic Institute for the Study of Innovation, Research and Education), Oslo, https://www.nifu.no/publications/996161/. [17]

Johanson, R. (2009), *A Review of National Training Funds,*, The World Bank, Washington DC, http://documents.worldbank.org/curated/en/893311468178131914/A-review-of-national-trainingfunds. [19]

Kuczera, M. (2017), "Incentives for apprenticeship", *OECD Education Working Papers*, No. 152, OECD Publishing, Paris, http://dx.doi.org/10.1787/55bb556d-en. [10]

Kuczera, M. (2017), "Striking the right balance: Costs and benefits of apprenticeship", *OECD Education Working Papers*, No. 153, OECD Publishing, Paris, http://dx.doi.org/10.1787/995fff01-en. [5]

Leiser, M. and S. Wolter (2017), "Empirical evidence on the effectiveness of social public procurement policy: The case of the Swiss apprenticeship training system", *Labour*, Vol. 31/2, pp. 204-222, http://dx.doi.org/10.1111/labr.12089. [18]

Leuven, E. and H. Oosterbeek (2004), "Evaluating the effect of tax deductions on training", *Journal of Labor Economics*, Vol. 22/2, pp. 461-488, http://dx.doi.org/10.1086/381257. [11]

Mühlemann, S. (2016), "The cost and benefits of work-based learning", *OECD Education Working Papers*, No. 143, OECD Publishing, Paris, https://doi.org/10.1787/5jlpl4s6g0zv-en. [4]

Mühlemann, S. et al. (2007), "An empirical analysis of the decision to train apprentices", *Labour*, Vol. 21/3, pp. 419-441, http://dx.doi.org/10.1111/j.1467-9914.2007.00379.x. [8]

Müller, N. and F. Behringer (2012), "Subsidies and levies as policy instruments to encourage employer-provided training", *OECD Education Working Papers*, No. 80, OECD Publishing, Paris, http://dx.doi.org/10.1787/5k97b083v1vb-en. [12]

OECD (2010), *Learning for Jobs*, OECD Reviews of Vocational Education and Training, OECD Publishing, Paris, https://doi.org/10.1787/9789264087460-en. [3]

Pfeifer, H. (2016), *Firms' Motivation for Training Apprentices: An Australian–German Comparison*, National Centre for Vocational Education Research (NCVER), Adelaide, https://www.ncver.edu.au/research-and-statistics/publications/all-publications/firms-motivation-for-training-apprentices-an-australian-german-comparison. [15]

Reed, D. et al. (2012), *Effectiveness Assessment and Cost-Benefit Analysis of Registered Apprenticeship in 10 States*, U.S. Department of Labor, Employment and Training Administration, Washington, https://wdr.doleta.gov/research/FullText_Documents/ETAOP_2012_10.pdf. [1]

SEFRI (2017), *Fonds En Faveur de La Formation Professionnelle Entrés En Vigueur Selon l'art. 60 LFPr." 2017.*, Secrétariat d'Etat à la formation, à la recherche et à l'innovation, http://www.sbfi.admin.ch/sbfi/fr/home/bildung/berufsbildungssteuerung-und--politik/berufsbildungsfinanzierung/fonds-en-faveur-de-la-formation-professionnelle-selon-art--60-lf.html. [14]

SEFRI (2009), *Évaluation Des Fonds En Faveur de La Formation Professionnelle*, Secrétariat d'Etat à la formation, à la recherche et à l'innovation, Confédération suisse, http://www.sbfi.admin.ch/sbfi/fr/home/bildung/berufsbildungssteuerung-und--politik/berufsbildungsfinanzierung/fonds-en-faveur-de-la-formation-professionnelle-selon-art--60-lf/evaluation-des-fonds-en-faveur-de-la-formation-professionnelle.html. [13]

Wacker, K. (2007), *Teure Neue Lehrstelle. Eine Untersuchung Zur Effizienz Des Blum- Bonus*, (New Expensive Apprenticeship. Analysing the Efficiency of the "Blum Bonus" Apprentice Funding Scheme), Austrian Chamber of Labour of Lower Austria, Wien. [6]

Westergaard-Nielsen, N. and A. Rasmussen (1999), *The Impact of Subsidies on Apprenticeship Training*, Centre for Labour Market and Social Research, Universitetsparken, https://www.researchgate.net/publication/265272135_The_impact_of_subsidies_on_Apprenticeship_Training. [2]

Wolter, S. and E. Joho (2018), *Apprenticeship Training in England – A Cost-effective Model for Firms?*, Education Policy Institute, Bertelsmann Stiftung and JP Morgan Chase Foundation, https://www.bertelsmann-stiftung.de/fileadmin/files/BSt/Publikationen/GrauePublikationen/LL_cost_benefit_study_England.pdf. [23]

Chapter 3. What is the right wage for apprentices?

This chapter focuses on the question of apprentice pay. It reviews the processes by which the wages of apprentices are determined across a number of OECD countries and the factors, such as training costs, productivity returns, competition from alternative employment and educational provision, which explain variation in earnings. The chapter looks at the cost-benefit balance to employers and to youth and adults considering apprenticeships. It identifies the need for special measures to ensure that apprenticeships are financially attractive to older learners.

The statistical data for Israel are supplied by and under the responsibility of the relevant Israeli authorities. The use of such data by the OECD is without prejudice to the status of the Golan Heights, East Jerusalem and Israeli settlements in the West Bank under the terms of international law.

Issues and challenges

Governments have limited influence on apprentice wages

The issue of apprentice wages is different from other issues discussed in this report, as government influence is relatively limited. Governments do not commonly define how much apprentices earn, instead, apprentice wages are typically set through a process of collective bargaining or agreed on an individual basis between an employer and the apprentice. However, governments can influence apprentice wages in several ways, such as setting minimum wages for apprentices, offering employers financial incentives to reduce the wage burden (see more in Chapter 2), or offering apprentices other financial support to reduce their wage expectations. The analysis presented below may also inform those involved in collective bargaining and individual employers.

Apprentice wages affect employer provision of training places

When employers offer apprenticeships, apprentice wages are the largest part of the costs incurred by employers and therefore a major determinant of the cost-benefit balance of apprenticeships to firms. Even in countries where apprentice wages are relatively low (e.g. Austria, Germany and Switzerland, see Table 3.1), they range between half and two-thirds of total costs. Data in many other countries are patchy, but the share of apprentice wages in total costs is likely to be even higher in countries where apprentice wages are relatively high. For example, a case study in the United States found that apprentice wages (and benefits) accounted for 70% of apprenticeship costs (Helper et al., 2016[1]).

Table 3.1. Apprentice wages in selected OECD countries

Country	Average apprentice wages as % of skilled worker wages	Wages paid by employers during off-the-job period	Share of apprentice wage cost in total cost of apprenticeship to employers
Austria	On average 50%	Yes	57% in the first year, 72% in the third year (Schlögl and Mayerl, 2016[2])
Denmark	30-70%	No[1]	n.a.
Germany	25-33%	Yes	About 62%
Norway	30-80%	No	n.a.
Switzerland	On average 20%	Yes	About 50% (Strupler, Wolter and Moser, 2012[3])

n.a. means not available.
1. In Denmark apprentices are paid during the off-the-job period from a levy fund.
Source: Kuczera, M. (2017[4]), "Striking the right balance: Costs and benefits of apprenticeship", *OECD Education Working Papers*, No. 153, http://dx.doi.org/10.1787/995fff01-en.

Apprentice wages help match supply and demand

Just like in the labour market, apprentice wages send a signal to potential applicants, making some choices more attractive than others and helping match supply to demand. Research shows that apprentice wages affect the perceived status of an occupation among potential apprentices (Ulrich, 2016[5]). In principle, if an employer faces skills shortages or struggles to attract apprenticeship candidates, it will be willing to offer higher wages. Such signals may be expressed at the individual firm level, for example in Switzerland, where apprentice wages are determined mostly by the market some sectoral bodies provide recommendations for minimum wages but research shows that apprentice wages

Figure 3.1. Average costs and benefits per apprentice during an apprenticeship in Germany (EUR)

By field of training, 2012/13

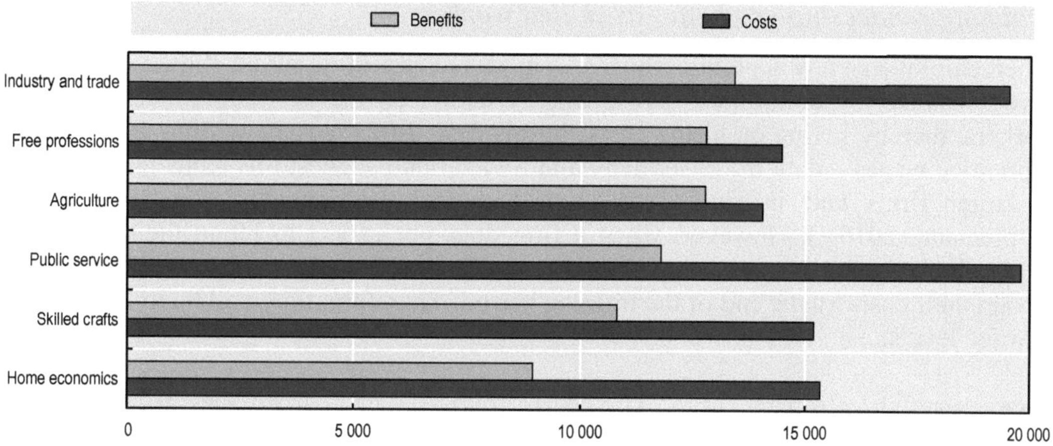

Source: Adapted from Mühlemann, S (2016[7]), "The cost and benefits of work-based learning", *OECD Education Working Papers*, No. 143, https://doi.org/10.1787/5jlpl4s6g0zv-en.

StatLink http://dx.doi.org/10.1787/888933828429

The evolution of apprentice productivity varies across occupations

Apprentices do not work as well and as fast as experienced workers, especially at the beginning of their apprenticeship. However, their productivity relative to skilled workers gradually increases throughout the programme. The pace of improvement varies across occupations (see Chapter 4): in some occupations, apprentices can be productive relatively quickly, while in others they will need lengthy training before being able to contribute to production. Apprentice wages typically increase according to a pre-defined scale over the duration of training to reflect increasing productivity.

Apprentice wages will not mirror apprentice productivity at each point in time, but wage (and other) costs and productive benefits should either roughly balance out over the whole apprenticeship period, or balance out once longer-term recruitment benefits are taken into account. For example, data from Germany and Switzerland show that at the initial stages, apprentices are paid above their productivity. At this stage, they spend a lot of time in training and their productive work involves mainly unskilled tasks. The situation reverses at the final stages of the programme, when apprentices are paid below their productivity. In Switzerland, research estimates that apprentices are 70% as productive as skilled workers during the last year of the apprenticeship programme, while their wages amount to 20-30% of skilled worker wages (SKBF, 2011[8]; Federal Statistics Office (FSO), 2016[9]). This final period compensates for the initial investment.

Policy argument 2: The room for employers to obtain benefits after the end of an apprenticeship varies by occupation and firm size

Firms are likely to be more responsive to wage levels if they do not expect to retain apprenticeship graduates as skilled workers

When employers view apprenticeships as a means of recruiting future skilled labour, they have a chance to recoup their investment by taking on the best apprentices as skilled workers, thereby saving on hiring costs. In this case, firms may be willing to pay higher apprentice wages – data from Germany and Switzerland suggest this tends to be the case in larger firms and in firms with high technical requirements (Kuczera, 2017[4]; Mühlemann, 2016[7]). However, when a firm does not expect to retain their apprentice after completion, or is uncertain about the possibility of doing so, they will be keen to recoup their costs by the end of the training period. Therefore, they will be more sensitive to wage levels.

Apprentice wages should also reflect the characteristics of apprentices and policy priorities

Apprentice wages need to be low enough to encourage companies to offer apprenticeships, but high enough to attract apprentices. From the point of view of potential apprentices, the attractiveness of the apprentice wage depends on their needs and how the apprenticeship compares to alternative career pathways available to them.

- Where youth apprentice wages are low, governments should ensure that they are balanced by extensive benefits to the young apprentice in terms of the quality of the learning opportunities with the employer.
- When policy efforts aim to increase the use of adult apprenticeships, measures should be devised to ensure that apprentice income is sufficient to make apprenticeships affordable for adults. This should be based on analysis of the relevant costs and benefits of particular target groups (e.g. by employment status or age) and may include financial support, on top of wages, for adult apprentices.

Policy argument 1: The optimal wage depends on the costs and outcomes of alternative learning pathways

Apprentices are more likely to accept lower wages if they expect good returns later on

When a young person still in the initial school system, or an adult in search of a better career, considers different options, one of the key questions will be how the costs involved compare to outcomes related to their future careers, including chances of finding employment, working conditions and wages – or more precisely, expectations and perceptions of such outcomes (career guidance and information are discussed in Chapter 7).

Comparative international evidence on apprenticeship outcomes relative to alternative pathways is patchy, but data from the Survey of Adult Skills, a product of the Programme for the International Assessment of Adult Competencies (PIAAC), provide some insights into outcomes in Austria, Canada, Denmark, Germany and Norway (see Figure 3.2). These results take into account the level of basic skills, so that the labour market returns identified do not reflect differences in basic skills. In all five countries, apprenticeship graduates are less likely to be unemployed than those without upper secondary education, and are as likely to be employed as those with post-secondary qualifications (Kuczera, 2017[4]). Wage returns are also promising: in all five countries, young apprenticeship graduates earn more than similar adults with academic upper secondary education (but no further studies). At the same time, apprenticeship graduates appear to earn less than those with post-secondary or tertiary qualifications, except in Canada and Norway where the difference is not statistically significant (Kuczera, 2017[4]).

Higher wage premiums may reflect various effects in addition to the impact of programmes on job-relevant skills. Some wage differences may result from pre-existing differences between learners who end up in different types of programmes – for example, those who pursue university studies may have better academic skills at the outset than those who decide on an apprenticeship. Even if the programmes pursued did not further develop those skills, university graduates would end up earning higher wages, and higher level qualifications may signal those skills to employers. Some apprenticeship graduates continue to higher levels of education (e.g. around 10% in Germany). Their outcomes, captured by the category post-secondary and tertiary, partly reflect outcomes from an apprenticeship. These biases mean that it is difficult to assess the potential returns where it matters most, i.e. to an individual, probably with mid-level or weaker school results deciding whether to pursue academic upper secondary education or an apprenticeship.

Figure 3.2. The wage premium for apprenticeship graduates

16-35 year-olds not in education, by highest level of qualification (excluding foreign qualifications)

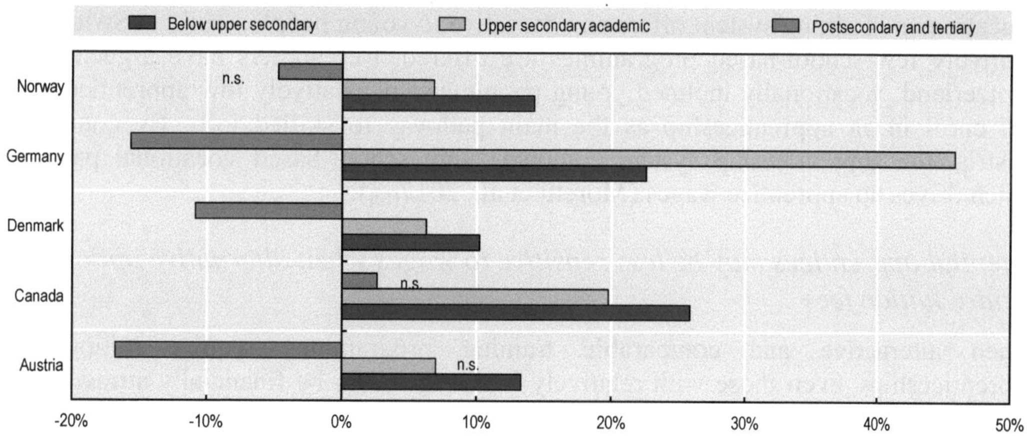

Note: Coefficients from the ordinary least squares (OLS) regression of log hourly earnings. Coefficients adjusted for numeracy skills, age, gender and firm size. Wage outliers (wages above the 99th percentile or below the 1st percentile) were dropped. Post-secondary and tertiary programmes include programmes at ISCED 4 A and B, ISCED 5 and ISCED 6 level. Upper secondary academic refer to programmes at ISCED 3 level that are longer than two years and those at ISCED 4C that are not vocational. For the definition of apprenticeship graduates see Annex A. n.s.: result is not statistically significant ($p > 0.05$).
Source: Kuczera, M. (2017[4]) "Striking the right balance: Costs and benefits of apprenticeship", *OECD Education Working Papers*, No. 153, https://doi.org/10.1787/995fff01-en.

StatLink http://dx.doi.org/10.1787/888933828448

Figure 3.2 shows how much apprenticeship graduates earn compared to those who have pursued other pathways. For example, for Norway the dark blue bar shows that apprenticeship graduates earn 7% more than those whose highest qualification is at academic upper secondary level. The light blue bar shows that apprenticeship graduates earn 14% more than those who completed only lower secondary education or less. The medium blue bar with the "n.s." sign indicates that the data do not reveal a statistically significant difference in wages between apprenticeship graduates and post-secondary or tertiary graduates.

Apprenticeships need to compete effectively with other programmes

Individuals will only choose an apprenticeship if the expected benefits (e.g. better employment chances, higher wages and better working conditions) justify the costs involved. To be attractive, apprenticeships also need to be at least as good, in terms of returns on investment, as alternative pathways. Depending on the country and individual context, alternatives will vary. Where apprenticeships are part of upper-secondary education and training (such as in most European countries), school-based vocational or academic programmes are the most likely alternative. In countries where apprenticeships build on basic schooling (such as in the United States), the alternatives are post-secondary education or entering the labour market. Those options will yield different benefits at different costs.

Competition from free school-based programmes can drive up apprentice wages

In countries where apprenticeships compete with school-based programmes, higher wages can make apprenticeships more attractive to young people. For example, Austria and Switzerland have apprenticeship schemes that are relatively similar by international standards. One important difference is that in Austria, the school-based vocational education and training system offers an alternative to young people, while in Switzerland, relatively few school-based programmes are offered. Researchers have argued that in Switzerland, vocationally inclined young people accept relatively low apprentice wages and enrol in an apprenticeship as the main pathway to skilled jobs. By contrast, in Austria, the apprenticeship system competes with school-based vocational pathways, which drives up apprentice wages (Moretti et al., 2017[10]).

Potential apprentices may be less sensitive to wages when alternative options require tuition fees

When alternative and comparable training programmes require tuition fees, apprenticeships, even those with relatively low wages, can be financially attractive. For example, in the United States, advocates of apprenticeships often argue that they offer an alternative to college degrees, allowing people to develop job-relevant skills without accumulating debt. While college education requires the payment of tuition fees, classroom instruction delivered during apprenticeships is usually free to apprentices, as employers either provide it in-house or cover tuition costs in community colleges (Helper et al., 2016[1]).

Policy argument 2: The optimal wage will be higher for adult apprentices

Adult apprentices have higher wage expectations

The reservation wage (the lowest wage a potential apprentice would be willing to accept) depends on both environmental factors (e.g. labour market tightness) and individual characteristics. Younger people have lower reservation wages because their immediate needs are low if they still live with their parents, because they expect to recoup their investment in an apprenticeship over their lifetime, and because the usual alternative to an apprenticeship is a school-based programme that offers no wage. However, for adults, the most likely alternative to an apprenticeship is full-time employment (or the prospect of it) with an unskilled wage at minimum. Adults often need to cover living costs and have family responsibilities, which means that many cannot afford to live on relatively low apprentice wages for several years. Adults also have fewer years of career left ahead of them than teenagers, so they have less time to recoup their investment (Mühlemann, forthcoming[11]). The combination of these factors means that for many adults, an apprenticeship will only be affordable if it offers relatively high wages during the training period.

Adult apprentices are also more productive than younger apprentices

The wage expectations of adult apprentices may be matched by employer willingness to pay higher wages if they consider that adults will be more productive during an apprenticeship than a younger candidate. Adult apprentices sometimes have years of work experience, including some in the relevant sector or within the same company. As adults often make use of apprenticeships to upskill or reskill, it is relevant to question whether provision should be significantly different from that aimed at young people.

Policy argument 3: In countries with large youth apprenticeships, adults in search of a second chance may struggle to find a suitable placement

Adults in search of a second chance may struggle to compete with young applicants

The role that apprenticeships play in a country's skills system is an important contextual feature. In countries with large youth apprenticeship systems (e.g. Germany and Switzerland), adults in search of an apprenticeship will be competing with teenagers. These adults will include some who have completed general education (even tertiary education) and are likely to be very attractive in the eyes of potential employers. However, some will be those who missed their first chance as teenagers and who will be looking to an apprenticeship as a second chance, having started their working life without a qualification. The mere fact of looking for a second chance may send a negative signal to potential employers about their skills, making them a less attractive candidate. Those who have useful work experience may find employers willing to pay them higher apprentice wages. But for those with a troubled work history, higher wage expectations are likely to create a hurdle, as employers will often prefer cheaper young apprentices who do not have a history of dropout. The implication is that in countries with large youth apprenticeship systems, adults who seek an apprenticeship as a second chance training programme are likely to struggle to find employers willing to meet their higher wage expectations. In such contexts, some countries have chosen to provide financial support to adult apprentices so that they can cover their living expenses without expecting employers to offer high apprentice wages (see Box 3.1).

The situation is different in countries where youth apprenticeships are uncommon, and where apprenticeships are one of the pathways to skilled jobs available to young (or indeed older) adults. In such contexts, most adults in search of an apprenticeship will be looking for a training opportunity, rather than a second chance. In countries where apprenticeships mostly serve adults (e.g. Canada and the United States), many adults work at the same firm that takes them on as an apprentice. For the firm, apprenticeships then become a tool for employee training. As they were paying regular employee wages to the apprentice before the training period, they will be willing to pay relatively high wages during the apprenticeship programme.

Employers may be more willing to consider adults if applicants are hard to find

Even in countries with large youth apprenticeship systems, employers will be more willing to take on adult apprentices if they struggle to find well-prepared young candidates. This is the case in Germany, where, partly for demographic reasons, apprenticeship positions in some areas and occupations remain unfilled because of the lack of suitable candidates. Similarly, in Israel, where apprenticeships remain very small in scale, employers face skills shortages and struggle to find apprenticeship candidates in the tight labour market, so the government has designed tools that complement adult apprentices' income during training.

Box 3.1. Special measures for adult apprentices

In **Germany,** the initiative *Zukunftsstarter* is designed to promote apprenticeships among adults aged 25 to 35 in response to skills shortages and a lack of young apprentices in some sectors. Individuals may receive financial support for education expenses, travel, childcare, tutoring, and subsistence during the training. Apprentices receive a grant upon passing mid-term and final examinations.

Israel has financial incentives for adults who wish to upskill, including subsidies that compensate for lost earnings. In *Class in the Workplace,* participants are eligible for a subsidy of NIK 1 500 (New Israeli Sheqel) and a grant upon passing mid-term and final examinations. *Starter* participants receive NIK 1 500 in the first stage of programmes provided in a college. The subsidy amounts to around one-third of the minimum wage.

In **Switzerland,** the earnings of adult apprentices are negotiated between the apprentice and their employer within the constraints of cantonal law. Typically, adult apprentices earn around two-thirds of the unskilled worker wage, compared to one-fifth for younger apprentices. Those under 35 can apply for a scholarship of a maximum CHF 12 000 (Swiss franc) per year, about equivalent to two and half times the median monthly wage of an unskilled worker. In some cases they are eligible for social assistance. Additional financial assistance is available to those who are unemployed.

Source: Ben Rabi, D. et al. (2017[121]), *Apprenticeship and Work-Based Learning in Israel. Background Report* (unpublished); Mühlemann, S. (forthcoming[111]), *Apprenticeship Training for Adults: Theoretical Considerations and Empirical Evidence for Selected OECD Member Countries.*

Conclusion

This chapter asks what is the right wage for an apprentice and concludes that wages need to be low enough to encourage employers to offer apprenticeships, but high enough to attract apprentices. Apprentice wages should vary to reflect the different costs and benefits incurred by employers across different forms of apprenticeship. Governments should resist imposing an overall level of apprentice wage, but should consider setting minimum wages to protect individuals from exploitation. Wages should be set by employers, or by sector, or occupation, within collective bargaining in recognition of the attractiveness of alternative education and employment options open to young people. Governments should recognise that financial barriers may prevent apprenticeships being attractive to older workers and consider remedial special measures, including grants for apprentices.

References

Ben Rabi, D. et al. (2017), *Apprenticeship and Work-Based Learning in Israel. Background Report (unpublished).* [12]

Federal Statistics Office (FSO) (2016), "Gross income from employement per year from employed persons according to economic activity status, group of occupation, workweek percentage and gender", in *Swiss Labour Force Survey*, Federal Statistical Office, https://www.bfs.admin.ch/bfs/en/home/statistics/catalogues-databases/tables.assetdetail.276590.html (accessed on 18 October 2016). [9]

Helper, S. et al. (2016), *The Benefits and Costs of Apprenticeship: A Business Perspective*, Case Western Reserve University, US Department of Commerce, Economics and Statistics Administration, http://www.esa.gov/sites/default/files/the-benefits-and-costs-of-apprenticeships-a-business-perspective.pdf. [1]

Kuczera, M. (2017), "Striking the right balance: Costs and benefits of apprenticeship", *OECD Education Working Papers*, No. 153, OECD Publishing, Paris, http://dx.doi.org/10.1787/995fff01-en. [4]

Moretti, L. et al. (2017), "So similar and yet so different: A comparative analysis of a firm's cost and benefits of apprenticeship training in Austria and Switzerland", *IZA Discussion Paper Series*, No. 11081, IZA - Institute of Labor Economics, Bonn, http://ftp.iza.org/dp11081.pdf. [10]

Mühlemann, S. (2016), "The cost and benefits of work-based learning", *OECD Education Working Papers*, No. 143, OECD Publishing, Paris, https://doi.org/10.1787/5jlpl4s6g0zv-en. [7]

Mühlemann, S. (forthcoming), *Apprenticeship Training for Adults: Theoretical Considerations and Empirical Evidence for Selected OECD Member Countries.* [11]

Mühlemann, S., P. Ryan and S. Wolter (2013), "Monopsony power, pay structure, and training", *ILR Review*, Vol. 66/5, pp. 1097-1114, http://dx.doi.org/10.1177/001979391306600504. [6]

Schlögl, P. and M. Mayerl (2016), *Betriebsbefragung zu Kosten und Nutzen der Lehrausbildung in Österreich*, (Company Survey on Costs and Benefits of the Apprenticeship Training in Austria, Interim Report), Austrian Institute for Vocational Training Research (öibf), Wien, http://www.bmwfw.gv.at/Berufsausbildung/Ingenieurwesen/Documents/endbericht_betriebsbefragung_oeibf.pdf. [2]

SKBF (2011), *Swiss Education Report 2010*, Swiss Coordination Centre for Research in Education, Aarau, http://www.skbf-csre.ch/fileadmin/files/pdf/bildungsmonitoring/Education_Report_2010.pdf. [8]

Strupler, M., S. Wolter and M. Moser (2012), *Die duale Lehre : eine Erfolgsgeschichte - auch für die Betriebe : Ergebnisse der dritten Kosten-Nutzen-Erhebung der Lehrlingsausbildung aus der Sicht der Betriebe*, (Dual Training: A Success Story for Companies: Results of the 3rd Cost-benefit Survey in the Eyes of Entreprises), Rüegger. [3]

Ulrich, J. (2016), "Berufsmerkmale und ihre Bedeutung für die Besetzungsprobleme von betrieblichen Ausbildungsplatzangeboten ("Job characteristics and their correlation with staffing problems of training places on offer")", *Berufsbildung in Wissenschaft und Praxis* 4. [5]

Chapter 4. How long should an apprenticeship last?

This chapter addresses the question of apprenticeship duration: how long an apprenticeship should last. It sets out the importance of duration within apprenticeship design to employers, apprentices and the state, and describes the relationship between duration and skill accumulation. It also explores distinctions between young and adult apprentices in terms of apprenticeship duration, and focuses on tools developed by countries to adapt the length of provision in recognition of the educational experiences, prior learning and vocational experience commonly enjoyed by older workers.

Issues and challenges

The duration of programmes needs to ensure both clarity and flexibility

In some apprenticeship schemes, programmes are the same or at least of similar length. This has the benefit of clarity, but rigidity may mean that the framework will suit some occupations and individuals, but will be poorly adapted to others. At the same time, leaving duration to be agreed on a case-by-case basis may undermine the concept of the apprenticeship itself, as there will be little clarity about what it involves and it may simply refer to any kind of training contract negotiated with an employer. If apprenticeships are of variable length, what criteria should determine the variation? Should duration depend on the targeted occupation? On the qualification level associated with the apprenticeship? Or on the characteristics and background of the apprentice? This section discusses the implications of duration for different stakeholders and sets out a rationale for how duration may be determined, illustrated with examples of international policy and practice.

The duration of apprenticeships affects various stakeholders

The duration of apprenticeship programmes is of concern to employers, apprentices and governments. Employers provide training to their apprentices and benefit from their work during the work placement. Apprentices accept lower wages while in training, but expect higher wages on completion. While apprenticeship training goes on, governments support it in various ways, usually by paying for the school-based component, and often through financial incentives to employers.

The profile of the apprentice population is often diverse and changes over time

The skillset that apprentices have at the start of their programme depends on their background. When new apprentices are teenagers, they typically have a similar schooling background and little work experience. Adult apprentices often bring either relevant work experience or higher levels of general education. Typically, apprenticeship schemes have been built around the needs of the historic target population. However, the profile of the apprentice population within a country often changes over time. For example, in Australia, over recent years the share of teenagers among new apprentices fell from nearly 100% to less than half (Knight and Karmel, 2011[1]). In England (United Kingdom), the share of those aged 25 and over among new apprentices has increased sharply over the past ten years, from 18% in 2009 to 47% in 2016 (Powell, 2018[2]). In Germany, the share of new apprentices holding a general upper-secondary certificate grew from 16 to 28% between 2006 and 2015 (BMBF, 2008[3]; BMBF, 2017[4]). The resulting challenge for policy makers is to ensure that apprenticeship schemes are adapted to the skillset and learning needs of apprentices.

The potential of competence-based approaches is not fully exploited

For apprenticeships, as in other education and training programmes, much attention is given to the definition of a clear learning programme that covers duration and what is learnt as a means of ensuring that all learners acquire the same targeted skillset. However, learners develop skills at different speeds, and sometimes already know some of the course content. In many education and training programmes, there have been efforts to move away from programmes with fixed "seat time" towards an approach in which learning outcomes are the pivotal element, recognising that the time it takes to achieve those may differ from one learner to another. However, despite widespread enthusiasm for competence-based approaches, implementation is challenging, and the potential of such approaches often remains unrealised.

Competence-based approaches can be especially useful to partially-skilled adults

Some adults have vocational skills but no qualifications reflecting these skills. Not holding a qualification creates a barrier to access jobs or to career progression when an occupation is licensed or collective agreements define salary scales linked to qualification requirements. Even in other occupations, holding a qualification that certifies occupational skills will open access to jobs and allow for better working conditions, which would not be accessible otherwise.

Many adults cannot afford to pursue a full-length apprenticeship, but may be willing and able to devote some time to training towards a qualification. This chapter focuses on two such pathways: a shortened version of an apprenticeship, or access to the final qualifying examination usually taken by apprentices. The first will typically suit those who have some of the targeted skills, and the second will be adapted to those who have most of the targeted skills. For some there may be a choice between the two options.

For governments and social partners, the benefits of creating such pathways will be particularly significant where there is untapped potential in partially-skilled labour without recognised qualifications. This includes: unqualified individuals with skills acquired through work experience, individuals with a vocational qualification seeking a career change in a related field, and migrants with skills not recognised in the host country.

Apprenticeship duration should reflect the targeted occupation

Over the duration of an apprenticeship, apprentices need time to develop the targeted skillset, but once they have acquired these skills they have an interest in becoming a qualified skilled worker as soon as possible. Employers, on the other hand, need time to train apprentices on the job and put their newly developed skills to use by engaging them in productive work. This productive work, particularly in the later stages of an apprenticeship, typically compensates for an employer's earlier investment in training. How long it takes to develop occupational skills, and how those skills can be used in productive work, varies across occupations.

- The duration of apprenticeships should be adapted to reflect the targeted occupation, in particular how apprentice productivity evolves during training.
- In occupations that target a more complex skillset, and where more time is needed to master skills, a longer duration will be more appropriate.

Policy argument 1: The duration of an apprenticeship needs to be attractive to both employers and potential apprentices

Employers tend to bear net costs at the beginning and reap benefits at later stages

Early on in apprenticeship programmes, employers make an investment as apprentices know little and spend much of their time learning. As apprentices develop new skills, they can increasingly contribute to productive work and generate benefits for their employer. Firms start reaping net benefits at the point when apprentices produce more valuable output than they cost. This latter period is vital to the apprenticeship programme as it allows employers to recoup much of their initial investment. Employers can reap further benefits at the end of apprenticeship by retaining the best apprentices as skilled workers, thus saving on recruitment costs (see Chapter 1).

Apprentice wages affect the cost-benefit dynamic for employers

Apprentice wages normally represent the largest part of the costs of apprenticeships to employers (apprentice wages are discussed in detail in Chapter 3). The arguments in this section are based on the usual scenario where apprentices are paid less than regular workers. When apprentices earn nearly as much as regular workers, there is less room for employers to benefit from the work of highly skilled apprentices. In some cases, employers may even be keen to have their apprentice graduate quickly so that he or she can dedicate all their time to productive work, rather than spending some of their time at school or college, and so that they are allowed to perform skilled tasks on their own.

How apprentice wages evolve in relation to the productivity of apprentices is important. If apprentice wages increase faster than apprentice productivity, net costs to employers may even be higher towards the end. This is the case, for example, in Austria, where a sharp increase in apprentice wages in the last year of an apprenticeship is combined with slow productivity gains. As a result, employer costs increase faster over the period of an apprenticeship than the benefits from the productive work of apprentices (Schlögl and Mayerl, 2016[5]).

The interests of apprentices must be taken into consideration

If an apprenticeship lasts too long, apprentices spend a long time at the end of the programme learning nothing (as they are already fully skilled) but earning lower wages than they would as skilled workers. At that stage they would be better off working as regular workers. A long apprenticeship with little learning would therefore represent poor quality. The length of apprenticeship needs to be adapted to the targeted skillset: making it too short will fail to attract employer interest, making it too long will not be appealing to apprentices. What "too long" or "too short" means depends on the time needed to learn the skills of the target occupation.

Policy argument 2: The optimal length of an apprenticeship varies across occupations

It takes longer to learn the skills required in more technically complex occupations

The time needed for an apprentice to acquire the productivity level of experienced workers depends on the complexity of the skills involved, how good the firm is at training, and the apprentice's ability. One way of capturing this is to ask employers their perception of how well and how fast apprentices perform skilled tasks compared to a skilled worker. These questions were part of an employer survey in Germany and Switzerland, yielding data on the "relative productivity" of apprentices. For example, relative productivity of 50% means that it takes twice as long for an apprentice electrician to install a socket than it would a skilled worker. The results show a great deal of variation across occupations (see Figure 4.1), for example, an apprentice in retail can quickly become productive, while a would-be industrial mechanic needs more time to become competent at their job.

Figure 4.1. How productive are apprentices at the start and at the end?

Relative productivity of apprentices, by occupation

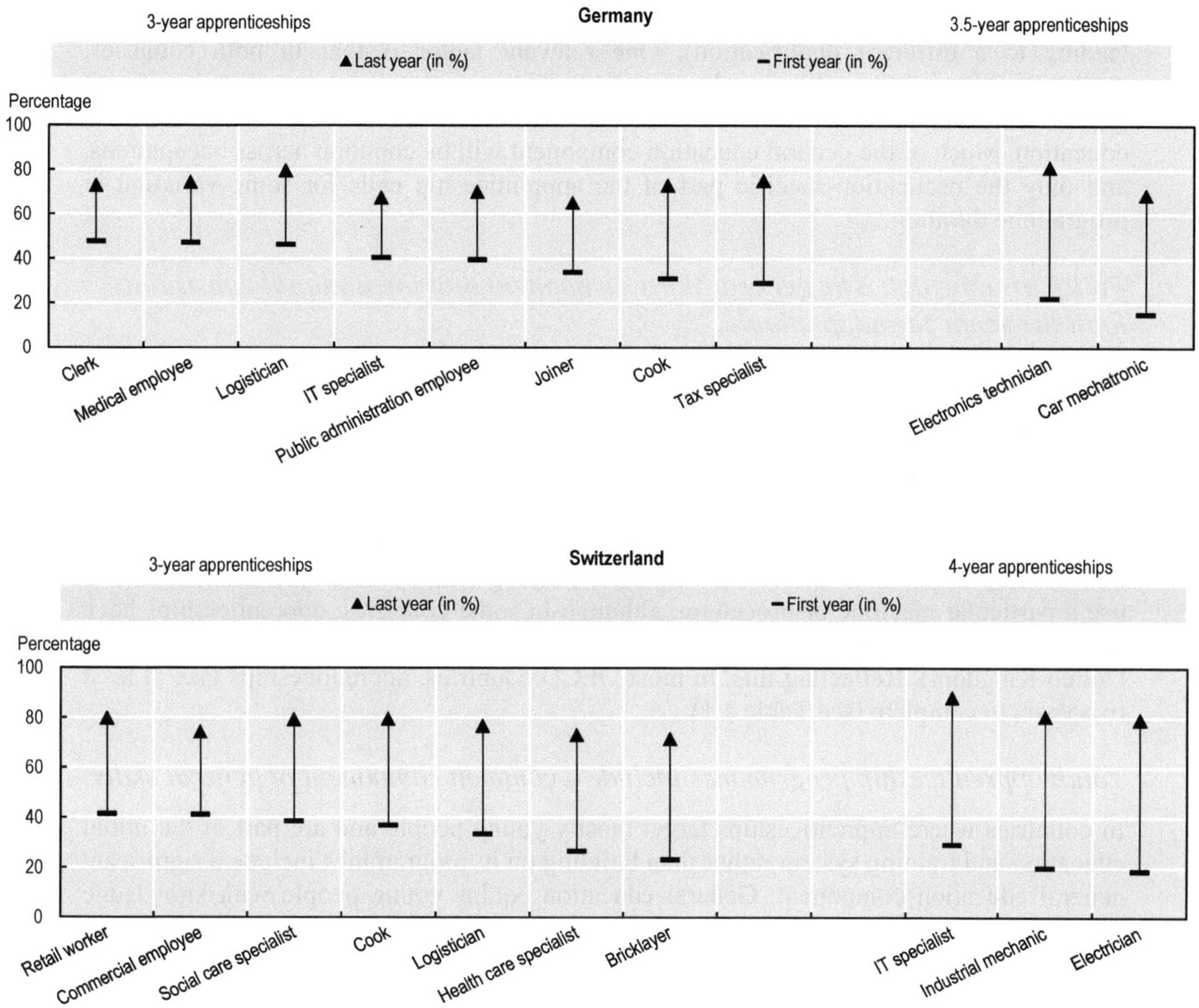

Note: Reference year 2009 for Switzerland, 2012/13 for Germany. Relative productivity is defined in comparison to the productivity of a skilled worker in the firm performing the same skilled tasks.
Source: Adapted from Mühlemann, S. (2016[6]), "The cost and benefits of work-based learning", *OECD Education Working Papers*, No. 143, https://doi.org/10.1787/5jlpl4s6g0zv-en.

StatLink http://dx.doi.org/10.1787/888933828467

Apprenticeships should last longer when becoming productive requires more time

The optimal duration for an apprenticeship will be typically longer in occupations in which it takes longer to learn the skills required. Evidence in Figure 4.1 shows a picture consistent with this idea: in both countries, apprenticeships last three years in "easier" occupations where apprentices' relative productivity is highest in the first year; while apprenticeships tend to last longer in occupations which are "harder" according to the first year relative productivity measure.

Only the occupation-specific component underpins variation in length by target occupation

The difference in duration across occupations remains relatively small in the countries illustrated by Figure 4.1 (although in Switzerland there are also two-year apprenticeship leading to a different qualification). One relevant factor is that in both countries, apprenticeships serve predominantly young people, so programmes include a significant general education component, such as literacy, numeracy, science, social studies and civic education. Much of the general education component will be common across occupations, and only the occupation-specific part of the apprenticeship calls for some variation in programme duration.

Policy argument 3: The general skills component and institutional constraints limit the scope for adaptation

Apprenticeships need to be long enough to prepare apprentices for a skilled occupation

Among vocational programmes that combine on-the-job and off-the-job components, apprenticeships are special in that they equip learners with the skillset needed for an occupation, and prepare them for a career. In this respect they are different from courses that develop a narrower skillset, for example training employees or job seekers how to use a particular machine or procedure, although in some countries, apprenticeships have been used for these narrower purposes (e.g. "dual fuel smart meter installer" in England, United Kingdom). Reflecting this, in most OECD countries, apprenticeships take at least two years to complete (see Table 4.1).

Youth apprenticeship programmes include a common component of general skills

In countries where apprenticeships target mostly young people and are part of the initial education and training system rather than building on it, programmes include a significant general education component. General education equips young people with knowledge and skills that are not directly relevant to a specific occupation, but that are applicable in most contexts of work and life. For example, in Germany, apprentices receive a minimum of 4 hours of general education per week,[1] amounting to about 480 hours of general education over a three-year apprenticeship (Hoeckel and Schwartz, 2010[7]). In Norway, apprentices receive 588 hours of general education in four-year apprenticeships (Norwegian Directorate for Education and Training, 2011[8]).

Apprenticeships in countries with more adult apprentices tend to contain limited general education

In countries where a large share of apprentices are adults, programmes tend to contain limited general education. For example, in England (United Kingdom), apprentices receive a minimum of 50-100 hours of general education (although some may receive more, depending on the target occupation) (Kuczera and Field, 2018[9]). In Australia, employer-led training packages, which define apprenticeships, contain a relatively limited amount of general education and have been criticised as inadequate (Knight and Karmel,

2011[1]). In the United States, the minimum requirement for registered apprenticeships refers to job-related education, without setting minimum requirements for education that is not occupation specific (United States Department of Labor (DOL), 2018[10]).

Table 4.1. Apprenticeship duration

Country	Programme duration
Austria	3-4 years
Denmark	3.5-4 years (typically)
England (United Kingdom)	On average 15 months (minimum 12 months)
Germany	2-3.5 years
Ireland	2-4 years
Netherlands	2-4 years
Norway	4 years (typically, shorter programmes target disadvantaged students)
Sweden	3 years
Switzerland	3-4 years (2-year programmes target disadvantaged students)
United States	1-6 years, mostly 4 years

Source: Adapted from Kuczera, M. (2017[11]), "Striking the right balance: Costs and benefits of apprenticeship", *OECD Education Working Papers*, No. 153, http://dx.doi.org/10.1787/995fff01-en; DOL (2018[10]), *United States Department of Labor - Frequently Asked Questions about the Apprenticeship Program*, www.dol.gov/featured/apprenticeship/faqs; Solas (2016[12]), *Apprenticeship: Real Life Learning*, www.apprenticeship.ie.

Institutional rigidities limit scope for adaptation

When apprenticeship programmes include a common general component (e.g. language, mathematics, history), these are typically delivered in schools or colleges. These institutions in turn organise their work in terms or semesters, and some general courses may be shared across different apprenticeship programmes. How apprenticeship programmes are organised need to balance some degree of adaptation to each target occupation and the necessity to ensure efficient delivery of school or college-based components.

The design of schemes can build on implicit knowledge among sectoral representatives

The information base used to set the duration of an apprenticeship programme for a specific occupation is diverse. It includes the complexity of the skills required, the usual initial skillset and other typical characteristics of apprentices, and how good firms are at training. There is a great deal of relevant experience and implicit knowledge among employers, workers and vocational schools and colleges. An electrician or a trainer will usually know how long it takes approximately for an 18-year-old apprentice to become sufficiently competent to work as a qualified electrician. The active involvement of sectoral representatives can bring this implicit knowledge into the design of apprenticeship schemes. It is widely accepted that the engagement of employers in the design of work-based learning schemes is key to successful implementation. At the same time, it is important to ensure that the interests of apprentices are also reflected in the design of apprenticeship programmes – this is often implemented through the involvement of trade unions, as well as regulations for quality assurance.

Some flexibility in duration should be allowed to accommodate for different starting points and learning speeds of apprentices

Apprenticeship schemes are typically built around the needs of the main target population. However, some apprentices have a different background, for example, adults starting an apprenticeship in a country with a large youth apprenticeship system. The profile of the apprentice population within the same country can also change, for example through migration, creating a need to adapt schemes to the learning needs of apprentices.

Individuals who have some of the skills targeted by an apprenticeship programme can benefit from the possibility of adjusting the length of the programme to reflect some degree of prior learning. Policy options include:

- Encourage the possibility of accelerated completion to recognise that some adult apprentices already have many general and occupation-specific skills. This may be supported by creating framework conditions for apprentices with relevant work experience, rather than leaving everything to individual negotiations.
- Ensure that the package associated with shorter apprenticeships is attractive to both employers and apprentices.

Policy argument 1: Starting points and learning speeds differ

Some apprentices have completed higher levels of general education, whereas others may have gaps in their general skills

In countries with large youth apprenticeship schemes, most new apprentices have a similar schooling background as they have recently completed lower secondary education. Adult apprentices, on the other hand, often have diverse general skills and learning needs. Some spent their teenage years completing general upper secondary education, and therefore already have the package of general skills included in apprenticeship programmes. Others may have left school with lower level qualifications and spent years away from classrooms and will need to refresh or fill gaps in their general skills.

Adults with relevant work experience have some of the targeted occupational skills

New apprentices who are older often have years of work experience, including some relevant to their training. They may have some but not all of the occupational skills for the target occupation, and often will need less time than an average apprentice to master the targeted skillset. For example, an adult training to be a cook with years of work experience in a restaurant may need to spend less time in on-the-job training.

Policy argument 2: Allowing for faster completion can benefit apprentices and the state

Shortening apprenticeships can lower the cost of qualification for apprentices

Pursuing an apprenticeship involves costs for apprentices, in particular opportunity costs – time spent earning apprentice wages instead of regular wages. In some cases, fees further increase costs for learners. For apprentices who already have some of the skills targeted by the programme, being able to complete the apprenticeship faster yields major benefits as it allows them to graduate and start earning skilled worker wages sooner. This can make the prospect of undertaking an apprenticeship more appealing to adults. The alternative to an apprenticeship for an adult is typically paid employment (rather than schooling, as for young people). As unskilled worker wages are typically higher than apprentice wages, many adults cannot afford to invest in their skills because they need to cover living costs and often have family responsibilities. The possibility of pursuing a shorter version of an apprenticeship, in recognition of their pre-existing skills, can make apprenticeship qualifications more accessible to adults.

Shortening apprenticeships can also benefit the state and society more broadly

Shortening the duration of an apprenticeship, in recognition of pre-existing skills, avoids wasting resources on teaching a person something they already know. Measures that allow apprentices with prior work experience to complete faster can also foster equity. They can provide a bridge and encourage those with good practical skills, but limited formal education, to return to education. Facilitating the recognition of skills through qualifications normally associated with apprenticeships can foster lifelong learning: the prospect of acquiring a formal qualification may motivate adults to invest time, energy and money in learning at work, which they may be less keen to do in the absence of some credit for the skills acquired.

Policy argument 3: Barriers that prevent the full use of reduced duration need to be addressed

Several countries allow for flexibility in the duration of apprenticeships

Various countries have created a regulatory framework that allows apprentices with relevant qualifications or work experience to complete their programme faster. The framework sets out the conditions to be met and the reductions allowed in different cases (see Box 4.1).

A different way of implementing flexibility is to adapt a general competence-based approach. Under such schemes only a theoretical or typical duration is defined, and an apprentice moves to the next stage of their training not after a pre-defined period of time, but when they have developed the required skills. Such approaches are used in Australia and in some programmes in the United States (see Box 4.2).

Employers may be reluctant to support a reduced duration if it means they lose out financially

Adjusting training duration in response to individual needs is possible in various countries, but barriers sometimes prevent its fuller use. Research in Australia found that the lack of employer support was a barrier to competency-based completion. Money seemed to be a major issue: faster progression means faster wage rises, and early completion means paying skilled worker wages instead of apprentice wages (Clayton et al., 2015[13]). Competence-based completion removes or reduces the period when apprentices are highly productive but receive an apprentice wage. However, this period is essential for employers, as the benefits during this time compensate for the costs incurred at the beginning, when apprentices were mostly learning and producing little.

Box 4.1. Shortening apprenticeship duration

Denmark

Adults aged 25 or more may complete an apprenticeship through two alternative pathways – an individual assessment decides which is the most suitable. Those with some relevant work experience or prior qualification follow a shortened basic course (school-based vocational education and training), a shortened main course (combining school and company-based training), and up to two years of on-the-job training. Those with at least two years of relevant experience follow only a shortened main course.

Source: MHES (2017[14]), *Admission to Vocational Education and Training (VET)*, https://ufm.dk/en/education/recognition-and-transparency/recognition-guide/admission-vet.

Germany

Adults aged 21 or more may have their training time reduced. Those with a secondary qualification (*Mittlere Reife*) can obtain a reduction of six months. Those with a general upper-secondary school-leaving exam, adults aged 21 and above, and those already holding a vocational qualification may obtain a 12-month reduction. An apprentice may take the final qualifying examination earlier if both the training firm and the vocational school attest above average performance.

Source: Mühlemann, S. (forthcoming[15]), *Apprenticeship Training for Adults: Theoretical Considerations and Empirical Evidence for Selected OECD Member Countries*.

United States

An apprentice can be awarded credit of up to 1 000 hours per year for prior learning and demonstrated competences. Apprentices must pursue at least half the time of the regular programme, with a minimum duration of six months required.

Source: Jones, D. and R. Lerman (2017[16]), *Starting a Registered Apprenticeship Program*, https://innovativeapprenticeship.org/wp-content/uploads/2017/06/Employer-Guide_June-2017.pdf.

Box 4.2. Competence-based completion

Australia

Apprentices may receive credit for existing skills and prior work experience. If an apprentice can demonstrate that they have acquired the required skill level, they may progress to the next stage of their training or complete the programme. Competency is assessed first by the "registered training organisation" (training provider). Then the training firm needs to confirm that the apprentice is able to apply the same skills in the workplace.

Source: Australian Government (2017[17]), *Australian Apprenticeships*, www.australianapprenticeships.gov.au.

United States

Registered apprenticeships may be competency-based or hybrid (others are time-based). In competency-based schemes, apprentices may complete faster or take extra time to develop the required competences. These schemes still have to comply with certain requirements regarding time spent on each major process. Hybrid apprenticeship programmes combine time-based and competency-based elements.

Source: DOL (2018[10]), *United States Department of Labor - Frequently Asked Questions about the Apprenticeship Program*, www.dol.gov/featured/apprenticeship/faqs.

Employers may support early completion if it does not have wage implications

The situation is different if early completion does not have wage implications. An apprentice who passes the qualifying exam continues to receive the wage set in the initial apprenticeship contract, i.e. lower than a qualified worker wage. In this case, there are no incentives for the employer to oppose reduced training duration. However, some of the benefits to individuals (a fast track to skilled worker wages) also disappear. Sometimes employers might support reduced training duration despite higher costs, for example, an adult apprentice may learn faster, be more mature and therefore more productive at work, so compensating for the higher costs. Employers may also be keen to fill a skilled worker vacancy, and faster completion can help them achieve that earlier.

Exploiting the potential of reduced duration requires that it works for all parties involved

One option is to let the apprenticeship market decide, and allow individual apprentices with relevant work experience to approach employers and negotiate a package (wages, time allocation, etc.) that is different from the standard apprenticeship package. In countries where apprentice wages (or apprentice minimum wages) are defined collectively (e.g. by occupation at the regional or national level), another approach is to define special conditions for apprentices who have relevant work experience – this may involve a different apprentice wage scale over the shortened duration of the apprenticeship. The key objective is to ensure that the package associated with shortened apprenticeships is attractive to both employers and individual apprentices.

Allow access to the final qualifying examination of an apprenticeship

Some individuals have acquired through work experience most of the skills expected of apprentices by the end of their training. Often some gaps remain and individuals may need to top up their existing skills with targeted courses or book learning, so that they have the same skillset as apprentices who have followed the standard programme.

- The final examination used to assess apprentices at the end of an apprenticeship can be used to check whether these individuals have acquired the targeted skillset, allowing them to obtain the qualification without pursuing the apprenticeship programme.
- Access to the final examination used in apprenticeships should be allowed to candidates who did not pursue the programme but can, because of relevant work experience, plausibly succeed at the examination.

Policy argument 1: Final examinations in apprenticeships can be used to validate skills regardless of how they were acquired

Some individuals have most of the skills targeted by an apprenticeship programme

For adults who have acquired most of the skills targeted by apprenticeships, even a shortened version of an apprenticeship may seem too long. For them, a more suitable path may involve topping up skills and filling in any gaps through targeted preparatory courses, and then taking a test to verify that they hold all the skills required. Potential beneficiaries include adults who have developed their skills through work experience, dropouts from apprenticeships, former apprentices who failed the final examination, and migrants who have worked in the target occupation abroad but whose qualification is not recognised in the host country.

Several countries allow access to the final apprenticeship examination

Under this model, a person may take the final qualifying examination without following the standard (or even adjusted version of) the apprenticeship programme. They are not apprentices, but they obtain the certification to which an apprenticeship normally leads. This is mostly used in countries with a long-standing tradition of apprenticeships (see Box 4.3). One reason might be that these countries have a well-developed standardised assessment that underpins the credibility of this route. In Austria, 15% of apprenticeship completers obtained their qualification by directly proceeding to final examinations in 2012 (Dornmayr et al., 2013[18]). In Norway 36% of apprenticeship qualifications (journeyman certificates) were delivered on the basis of an experience-based examination in 2015/16. Among adults aged 25 and above, experience-based examinations accounted for 47% of delivered qualifications (Bratsberg, Nyen and Raaum, 2017[19]). Such examinations were most common in health and childcare and construction, which together accounted for over 60% of experience-based examinations (Norwegian Directorate for Education and Training, 2016[20]). In Germany, 6% of all apprenticeship examinations were awarded following direct access to the examination in 2009. Over two-thirds of those who directly accessed the final examination were entitled in recognition of their work experience (BIBB, 2011[21]). In Switzerland, 3% of vocational qualifications were awarded following direct admission to the final examination in 2015, but among qualifications delivered to adults (aged 24 and above) direct admissions accounted for a quarter of qualifications (SERI, 2017[22]).

Box 4.3. Direct access to the final examinations associated with apprenticeship

Austria

Individuals aged 18 or over may directly apply for the final apprenticeship examination without enrolling as an apprentice. For this they must have relevant work experience, which means that they are very likely to hold skills similar to those of apprentices in the targeted occupation. Such skills can be acquired through internships, non-formal training in a company, other practical experience, or enrolling in schooling.

Source: Mühlemann, S. (forthcoming[15]), *Apprenticeship Training for Adults: Theoretical Considerations and Empirical Evidence for Selected OECD Member Countries*; Dornmayr, H. et al (2013[18]), *Lehrabschlussprüfungen in Österreich*, www.bmwfw.gv.at/Berufsausbildung/LehrlingsUndBerufsausbildung/Documents/Lehrabschlusspr%C3%BCfung.ibw-%C3%B6ibf%20Zwischenbericht%202013.pdf.

Germany

Individuals may take the final assessment of regular apprenticeship programmes without completing the programme itself (*Externenprüfung*). For this they must have worked in the target occupation at least for one and a half times as long as the length of the apprenticeship, and they must have performed skilled tasks. Relevant school qualifications may reduce or replace the required minimum work experience. Candidates may prepare for the assessment by themselves (e.g. taking tests from past years) or follow preparatory courses.

Source: BMBF (2017[23]), *Externenprüfung: Voraussetzungen, Beratung und Vorbereitung*, www.perspektive-berufsabschluss.de/de/501.php.

Norway

Candidates may obtain an experience-based trade certification (*praksiskandidat*) by taking the trade or journeyman's examination without pursuing an apprenticeship. The candidate must demonstrate comprehensive competence in the field and cover the objectives in the curriculum. The length of the candidate's work experience in the field must be equivalent to the length of the apprenticeship period plus 25%, and the candidate must pass a theoretical exam. Relevant previous education is recognised as practical training.

Source: Norwegian Centre for International Cooperation in Education (SIU) (2016[24]), "Vocational education and training in Europe – Norway", *Cedefop ReferNet VET in Europe reports*, http://libserver.cedefop.europa.eu/vetelib/2016/2016_CR_NO.pdf; Norwegian Directorate for Education and Training (2016[20]), *Skoleporten*, http://skoleporten.udir.no/rapportvisning/fag-og-yrkesopplaering/laeringsresultater/.

Switzerland

Adults with relevant work experience may access the final qualifying examination of an apprenticeship. This requires five years of work experience, of which professions determine a minimum period employed in the target occupation. While variation exists between professions, typically a minimum of three years employment in the occupation is required. Cantons provide advice to applicants about how to prepare for the examination, with preparatory courses available in some occupations. In all occupations, adults may pursue additional training by attending vocational schools or inter-company training centres.

Source: SERI (2017[221]), *Berufsabschluss für Erwachsene*, www.berufsbildungplus.ch/berufsbildungplus/berufsbildung/einstieg/erwachsene.html.

Rigorous assessments are the foundation of qualifications delivered without a mandatory training programme

When a qualification is delivered without programmatic requirements, its value in the labour market will depend on the credibility of the underlying assessments. Designing and implementing valid and reliable assessments is challenging, as skilled jobs require a very wide range of skills and knowledge (see Chapter 5 for a discussion of assessments in apprenticeships). In practice, measuring all the relevant learning outcomes can be very difficult, so it is reasonable to give some attention to other tools that can testify to a person's skills (such as the length and content of workplace experience and training courses pursued), at least as an adjunct to an examination that will inevitably leave some things out.

Policy argument 2: Such tools can help adults obtain a vocational qualification

Access to the final examination may offer second chances to low-qualified adults

In Norway, two-thirds of those who obtained a VET qualification based on experience-based examinations between 1998 and 2015 lacked an upper-secondary qualification at the outset. Research also found that those pursuing experience-based examinations had a similar socio-economic background to adults without upper-secondary education. Conversely, adults who pursued a regular apprenticeship programme had a similar socio-economic background to young people who had completed an apprenticeship. Data analysis drawing on nearly 20 years of register data suggests that experience-based examinations therefore serve as a tool to reduce educational inequalities (Bratsberg, Nyen and Raaum, 2017[19]).

Direct access to final examinations can serve as an alternative to regular apprenticeships

Direct access to final examinations offers a highly flexible route to an apprenticeship qualification. For example, a person might hold a regular (i.e. not apprenticeship) contract with their employer and prepare for the examination through learning on the job and off the job (e.g. preparatory courses). This arrangement might suit the profile and needs of adult learners and their employers: if training an adult under the apprenticeship framework is unattractive to employers, it may be preferable to offer access to the final examination supplemented by some preparatory courses. This might particularly suit the needs of adults in search of a vocational qualification in countries where the apprenticeship system is designed around the needs of young apprentices. This alternative pathway to an apprenticeship qualification is based on similar dynamics to regular apprenticeships in countries where most apprentices are adults. In these countries, apprentice wages tend to be higher or may even exceed the going minimum wage. For example, apprentice pay is much closer to unskilled pay for apprentices aged 18 and younger, and equal to the minimum wage for apprentices older than 19 in the United Kingdom; and in Canada, apprentice pay exceeds the minimum wage (Mühlemann, forthcoming[15]).

Conclusion

This chapter asks how long an apprenticeship should last and finds that duration should reflect the difficulty of the skills being learnt and the characteristics of the learner. Apprenticeship duration matters to the apprentice, employer and the state, and benefits are found when there is both clarity and flexibility in programme length. The duration of an apprenticeship needs to be adapted to the targeted skillset and reflect the cost-benefit analysis of both the employer and the apprentice: making it too short will fail to attract employer interest, making it too long will not be appealing to apprentices. The engagement of social partners in apprenticeship design can make it easier to balance different interests. For young apprentices, an apprenticeship forms part of initial education, and provision typically includes a significant proportion of general education alongside the learning of technical skills. By contrast, adults, including new migrants, often come to an apprenticeship with strong general education or relevant work experience, which deserve recognition. Countries have developed approaches to shorten the duration of apprenticeships for such learners or allow them to progress directly to a final qualifying exam. Such tools, when based on robust assessments, serve to build greater equity and efficiency into apprenticeship systems.

Note

[1] Apprentices spend at least 12 hours per week in a vocational school (Eurydice, 2018[25]), about a third of which is general education (BMBF, 2017[26]).

References

Australian Government (2017), *Australian Apprenticeships*, http://www.australianapprenticeships.gov.au (accessed on 30 August 2017). [17]

BIBB (2011), *Datenreport zum Berufsbildungsbericht 2011*, (Data Report for the Report on Vocational Education and Training for the Year 2011), Federal Institute for Vocational Training, Bonn, https://datenreport.bibb.de/media2011/Datenreport_2011.pdf. [21]

BMBF (2017), *Berufsbildungsbericht 2017*, (Report on Vocational Training 2017), Federal Ministry of Education and Research, Bonn, https://www.bmbf.de/pub/Berufsbildungsbericht_2017.pdf. [4]

BMBF (2017), *Duale Berufsausbildung Sichtbar Gemacht*, (Dual Vocational Education Made Visible), Federal Ministry of Education and Research, Bonn, http://www.bmbf.de/pub/Duale_Berufsausbildung_sichtbar_gemacht_Broschuere.pdf. [26]

BMBF (2017), *Externenprüfung: Voraussetzungen, Beratung und Vorbereitung*, (External Examination: Requirements, Consulting and Preparation), Federal Ministry of Education and Research, Bonn, http://www.perspektive-berufsabschluss.de/de/501.php. [23]

BMBF (2008), *Berufsbildungsbericht 2008*, (Report on Vocational Training 2008), Federal Ministry of Education and Research, Bonn, https://www.bmbf.de/pub/Berufsbildungsbericht_2008.pdf. [3]

Bratsberg, B., T. Nyen and O. Raaum (2017), *Fagbrev i voksen alder*, (Vocational Qualifications in Adulthood), https://www.idunn.no/spa/2017/01-02/fagbrev_i_voksen_alder. [19]

Clayton, B. et al. (2015), *Competency Progression and Completion: How is the Policy Being Enacted in Three Trades?*, https://www.ncver.edu.au/research-and-statistics/publications/all-publications/competency-progression-and-completion-how-is-the-policy-being-enacted-in-three-trades. [13]

Danish Ministry of Higher Education and Science (MHES) (2017), *Admission to Vocational Education and Training (VET)*, https://ufm.dk/en/education/recognition-and-transparency/recognition-guide/admission-vet (accessed on 30 August 2017). [14]

Dornmayr, H. et al. (2013), *Lehrabschlussprüfungen in Österreich*, (Final Apprenticeship Examinations in Austria), Institute for Research on Qualifications and Training of the Austrian Economy, Austrian Institute for Vocational Training Research, https://www.bmwfw.gv.at/Berufsausbildung/LehrlingsUndBerufsausbildung/Documents/Lehrabschlusspr%C3%BCfung.ibw-%C3%B6ibf%20Zwischenbericht%202013.pdf. [18]

Eurydice (2018), *Germany. Organisation of Vocational Upper Secondary Education*, https://eacea.ec.europa.eu/national-policies/eurydice/content/organisation-vocational-upper-secondary-education-20_en (accessed on 12 February 2018). [25]

Hoeckel, K. and R. Schwartz (2010), *OECD Reviews of Vocational Education and Training: A Learning for Jobs Review of Germany 2010*, OECD Reviews of Vocational Education and Training, OECD Publishing, Paris, http://dx.doi.org/10.1787/9789264113800-en. [7]

Jones, D. and R. Lerman (2017), *Starting a Registered Apprenticeship Program*, Urban Institute, https://innovativeapprenticeship.org/wp-content/uploads/2017/06/Employer-Guide_June-2017.pdf. [16]

Knight, B. and T. Karmel (2011), "Apprenticeships and traineeships in Australia", in Dolphin, T. and T. Lanning (eds.), *Rethinking Apprenticeships*, Institute for Public Policy Research, London, https://www.ippr.org/files/images/media/files/publication/2011/11/apprenticeships_Nov2011_8028.pdf. [1]

Kuczera, M. (2017), "Striking the right balance: Costs and benefits of apprenticeship", *OECD Education Working Papers*, No. 153, OECD Publishing, Paris, http://dx.doi.org/10.1787/995fff01-en. [11]

Kuczera, M. and S. Field (2018), *Apprenticeship in England, United Kingdom*, OECD Reviews of Vocational Education and Training, OECD Publishing, Paris, http://dx.doi.org/10.1787/9789264298507-en. [9]

Mühlemann, S. (2016), "The cost and benefits of work-based learning", *OECD Education Working Papers*, No. 143, OECD Publishing, Paris, https://doi.org/10.1787/5jlpl4s6g0zv-en. [6]

Mühlemann, S. (forthcoming), *Apprenticeship Training for Adults: Theoretical Considerations and Empirical Evidence for Selected OECD Member Countries*. [15]

Norwegian Centre for International Cooperation in Education (SIU) (2016), "Vocational education and training in Europe – Norway", *Cedefop ReferNet VET in Europe reports 2016*, http://libserver.cedefop.europa.eu/vetelib/2016/2016_CR_NO.pdf. [24]

Norwegian Directorate for Education and Training (2016), *Skoleporten*, http://skoleporten.udir.no/rapportvisning/fag-og-yrkesopplaering/laeringsresultater/ (accessed on 16 September 2016). [20]

Norwegian Directorate for Education and Training (2011), *Fag- og timefordelingen i grunnopplæringen Kunnskapsløftet*, http://www.udir.no/Upload/Rundskriv/2011/Udir-1-2011-Fag-ogtimefordeling_des2011.pdf. [8]

Powell, A. (2018), "Apprenticeship statistics: England", *Briefing Paper*, No. 06113, House of Commons Library, http://researchbriefings.parliament.uk/ResearchBriefing/Summary/SN06113#fullreport. [2]

Schlögl, P. and M. Mayerl (2016), *Betriebsbefragung zu Kosten und Nutzen der Lehrausbildung in Österreich*, (Company Survey on Costs and Benefits of the Apprenticeship Training in Austria, Interim Report), Austrian Institute for Vocational Training Research (öibf), Wien, http://www.bmwfw.gv.at/Berufsausbildung/Ingenieurwesen/Documents/endbericht_betriebsbefragung_oeibf.pdf. [5]

SERI (2017), *Berufsabschluss für Erwachsene*, (Professional Qualifications for Adults), Secretariat for Education, Research and Innovation, Bern, http://www.berufsbildungplus.ch/berufsbildungplus/berufsbildung/einstieg/erwachsene.html. [22]

Solas (2016), *Apprenticeship: Real life Learning*, http://www.apprenticeship.ie (accessed on 12 February 2018). [12]

United States Department of Labor (DOL) (2018), *United States Department of Labor - Frequently Asked Questions about the Apprenticeship Program*, http://www.dol.gov/featured/apprenticeship/faqs (accessed on 5 March 2018). [10]

Chapter 5. How to ensure a good learning experience at work?

The focus of this chapter is on the workplace as the location of apprentice learning. It describes how apprentices split their time between productive and non-productive tasks, and explores approaches, such as supervisor training and the management of work tasks, which can enable apprentices to integrate learning and productive work. The chapter concludes by reviewing the functions of final apprenticeship examinations, the training of examiners, and innovative means of assessing the full range of apprentice knowledge and skills. The function of summative apprenticeship examinations in confirming the skills of workers who receive exemptions from full programmes is also discussed.

The statistical data for Israel are supplied by and under the responsibility of the relevant Israeli authorities. The use of such data by the OECD is without prejudice to the status of the Golan Heights, East Jerusalem and Israeli settlements in the West Bank under the terms of international law.

Issues and challenges

Learning at work is a vital element in high-quality apprenticeships

Training delivered in workplaces is at the heart of apprenticeships. Workplaces provide a powerful learning environment that allow technical skills to be learnt on the latest equipment and under the guidance and supervision of practitioners who know how to use the equipment. Soft skills, such as teamwork and negotiation, are acquired in context following the example of experienced professionals.

The learning experience at work is a crucial determinant of the overall quality of an apprenticeship programme. This is because apprentices typically spend at least half of their time in a workplace (see Table 5.1), unlike in school-based vocational programmes where work-based learning, if offered, is a top-up to learning at school.

Table 5.1. How do apprentices spend their time?

	Time allocation	Share of productive work in time spent at the workplace
Austria	66% - workplace; 20% - off-the-job education and training; 14% - leave and sick days	83% spent on productive work
England (United Kingdom)	Up to 80% - workplace; minimum 20% off-the-job education and training	
Germany	56% - workplace; 29% - off-the-job education and training; 14% - leave and sick days	77% spent on productive work
Norway	Typically, two years spent at school followed by two years in the workplace	1 year of training 1 year of productive work
Switzerland	59% - workplace; 27% - off-the-job education and training; 14% - leave and sick days	83% of the time with the company is spent on productive work

Source: Kuczera, M. (2017[1]), "Striking the right balance: Costs and benefits of apprenticeship", *OECD Education Working Papers*, No. 153, http://dx.doi.org/10.1787/995fff01-en.

Apprentices may perform different types of tasks at work

A key question for apprenticeship programmes is how to allocate the time spent by apprentices in the workplace between different activities. The mix of activities needs to allow apprentices to develop the skills targeted by the programme, while being financially worthwhile for the firm. Apprentices may spend time in three types of task:

- **Non-productive activities**: activities of no direct productive value to the firm. This includes some types of learning (e.g. doing exercises or listening to a supervisor's explanations) and other activities (e.g. time spent in transport to visit a client).
- **Productive skilled activities**: tasks normally performed by a skilled worker. This may involve learning (e.g. practicing a technique while doing real work) or not (e.g. work using skills the apprentice already masters).
- **Productive unskilled activities**: tasks that can be done by an unskilled worker (e.g. cleaning a workshop). Performing such tasks does not develop technical skills, but it may develop soft skills, such as the ability to work in a team or time management.

The kind of tasks that apprentices perform impact their employer financially

What exactly apprentices do while in the workplace affects the balance of costs and benefits for employers. For example, a restaurant benefits when an apprentice cook peels potatoes (productive unskilled activities) and when they bake a soufflé (productive skilled activities), but gains no immediate benefits when the would-be cook is practicing skills that are not part of the production process, even though they are developing their skills (non-productive activities). The benefits associated with training (including those practice exercises) are realised by the firm later on, when apprentices put their newly developed skills into practice and perform skilled tasks. Instead of paying regular employees (with skilled worker wages) to perform the task, the apprentice can do the same but at lower wages.

There is a risk that apprentices are exploited as cheap unskilled labour

While it is possible for employers to benefit financially from teaching apprentices new skills, sometimes they could reap even more benefits by delivering little training and using apprentices as unskilled workers. This requires little investment from the firm, but, if the apprentice wage is low, would yield benefits associated with the productive unskilled work carried out by the apprentice. Simulations based on cost-benefit surveys show that Swiss employers could increase their net benefits by an average of EUR 22 000 per apprentice over the period of an apprenticeship if the apprentices performed only unskilled tasks while in the workplace [Wolter and Ryan (2011[2]) in Mühlemann (2016[3])].

Regulations are needed to ensure that all apprentices receive high-quality work-based learning

Relying on employers' interests in delivering training is not enough to ensure that all apprentices receive high-quality training at work: regulations are also needed. In countries with strong apprenticeship systems, regulations ensure that employers train their apprentices, rather than just exploiting them as cheap unskilled labour. This requires standards that define the skills apprentices should develop while in the workplace, employers that are able to deliver high-quality training, and rigorous assessments to check whether the apprentice has acquired the targeted skills.

Sometimes workplaces are used mainly to put skills into practice, and not enough as learning environments

As apprenticeships have evolved historically in different countries, the long-standing obligation on an employer to provide instruction has been augmented by off-the-job education and training and education provided by schools or colleges. In some countries, programmes also include training funded and organised by employers but offered in shared training centres (e.g. Germany and Switzerland). In most countries, learning in different settings makes for a valuable blend of complementary experience. However, in some apprenticeship schemes the training obligation of employers has been diminished, with expectations and regulations mostly focusing on training provided in school or college settings. For example, in England (United Kingdom), quality assurance focuses on off-the-job training provided by a registered training provider. Unless the training provider is the firm providing the apprenticeship, there is little expectation on employers to deliver training as part of the apprenticeship (Kuczera and Field, 2018[4]).

The training capacity of employers must be built and supported

The quality of the learning experience in workplaces has a huge impact on the overall quality of apprenticeships, as apprentices spend much (often most) of their time with an employer. However, while schools are built around the objective of teaching, workplaces are designed primarily to produce. Taking on and training apprentices, while continuing with day-to-day production activities, is demanding for employers.

- Training capacity should be supported, helping employers to deliver high-quality training to apprentices. This support may be facilitated through public policy, collective action by firms (e.g. sectoral bodies, employer organisations or unions) or a combination of both. Targeted training should be offered to apprentice supervisors.
- Stronger training capacity in workplaces benefits apprentices by ensuring that all have a high-quality learning experience at work, meaning that they can develop the technical and softer skills targeted by the programme that will equip them for successful careers.
- Employers can benefit by strengthening their training capacity through a better integration of apprentices into the production process. In firms that are better at training, apprentices develop skills faster. Where learning is better integrated into productive work, apprentices can practice and hone their skills, while also contributing to output.

Policy argument 1: Delivering high-quality apprenticeships requires strong management and training capacity

Training capacity underpins apprenticeship systems

Some employers may not feel able to train apprentices, and some are better than others at conducting training on the job. Training capacity depends on the training skills of apprentice supervisors, the quality of training methods and equipment, and the capacity to deal with the procedures associated with apprenticeships (such as administration and assessments). Such capacity is at the heart of the "apprenticeship tradition", and is well-established in countries and sectors with a long history of apprenticeships: supervisors were often trained as apprentices themselves, and firms know how to train in compliance with regulations and have the capacity to deal with related administrative tasks. A key implication is that the "apprenticeship tradition" can be gradually built (or indeed lost) over time. By supporting the training capacity of employers, apprenticeships can be promoted in countries with mostly school-based programmes, expanded into new economic sectors, or encouraged in types of workplaces that have previously been little engaged in apprenticeship provision.

Training capacity may be supported in various ways

Governments can enhance the training capacity of employers through a wide range of tools that help employers develop their training skills. Governments can also facilitate networking among employers to share knowledge and experience on how best to support, develop and make use of apprentices and training apprentice supervisors (further discussed below). Sharing some of the training responsibility can relieve the training burden on firms. This can be especially helpful to small firms that often lack the staff and training equipment to cover the entire curriculum (see country examples in Chapter 2).

Apprentice supervisors shape the learning experience of apprentices at work

Employees who supervise apprentices in the workplace have heavy responsibilities. New apprentices not only have to learn a range of technical skills, but also need to acquire a diverse set of soft skills regarding how they work with colleagues, relate to their boss, communicate with customers and sometimes handle conflict. Young apprentices are also learning how to deal with life in the workplace, and may also, as teenagers transitioning to adulthood, have to tackle personal problems that may include issues such as drug and alcohol abuse. Any one of these issues, if not well handled, could lead to the apprentice dropping out. Young apprentices from disadvantaged or troubled backgrounds, as discussed in Chapter 6, may face particular challenges.

Targeting training at apprentice supervisors can support high-quality training

Apprenticeship regulations in several countries require employers to be prepared to deliver an apprenticeship, with specific requirements for apprentice supervisors. When such requirements exist, apprentice supervisors are typically expected to hold proof of relevant technical and training skills. Targeted training for apprentice supervisors is mandatory in Germany, the Netherlands, the province of Ontario in Canada and Switzerland; it is optional in Norway (see Box 5.1). Evidence suggests that better prepared apprentice supervisors underpin high-quality training. In Germany, the temporary suspension of compulsory training for apprentice supervisors was associated with higher apprentice dropout rates and more complaints on behalf of companies about the performance of apprentices. In light of this experience, mandatory training for apprentice supervisors was reintroduced in 2009 after a six-year suspension (BIBB, 2009[5]).

Sometimes regulations are loose. In Australia, for example, apprentices are regular employees and the challenge is to ensure that they receive training in addition to tasks performed within the framework of their regular job. Some Australian states tackle this issue by requiring those supervising apprentices to be qualified for the task (Queensland Government, 2018[6]) In Israel, regulations set out competence requirements for apprentice supervisors, although these are not always respected as firms struggle to cover their costs (Kuczera, Bastianić and Field, 2018[7]).

Developing management capacity has broader benefits for employers

The capacity to train apprentices is similar to general management capacity. All workers are, in reality, partially rather than fully skilled, particularly in the context of technological change and innovation, where everyone is trying out new approaches and tasks. The job of managers is to guide and support staff and ensure that key immediate tasks are performed, while also deepening existing skills and developing new skills. This is a very challenging task, similar to that of someone supervising apprentices. The implication is that measures that develop employer capacity to manage apprentices will also assist their capacity to manage other staff.

Box 5.1. Training for apprentice supervisors

Canada: Apprentice supervisors in Canadian jurisdictions must be qualified journeypersons. For many trades in Canadian apprenticeship programmes, there is specified training time allotted for effective mentorship practices. This is often provided in the final period of apprenticeship in-school training periods so that when apprentices become certified journeypeople, they have an effective knowledge base to become good mentors.

Source: Government of Ontario (2017[8]), *Hire an Apprentice*, www.ontario.ca/page/hire-apprentice; Industry Training Authority (2017[9]), *Apprenticeships Who's Who*, www.itabc.ca/about-apprentices/apprenticeship-who%E2%80%99s-who.

Germany: Apprentice supervisors with an upper-secondary vocational qualification must pass the trainer aptitude examination, which verifies their ability to assess educational needs, plan and prepare training, assist in the recruitment of apprentices, deliver training, and prepare apprentices for the examination (BIBB, 2009[10]). Candidates typically prepare through "training for trainer" courses, which last 115 hours and are provided by chambers of commerce (BIBB, 2009[5]). The examination costs EUR 180, on average, while preparatory courses cost up to EUR 420. Candidates may be supported by their employers and can seek financial support from the state (TA Bildungszentrum, 2015[11]). Those with higher vocational qualifications are entitled to supervise apprentices, as master craftsperson programmes include this element.

Source: BIBB (2009[10]), "Ausbilder-Eignungsverordnung Vom 21 Januar 2009", Bundesgesetzblatt 5, www.bibb.de/dokumente/pdf/ausbilder_eignungsverordnung.pdf; BIBB (2009[5]), *Empfehlungen des Hauptausschusses des Bundesinstituts für Berufsbildung zum Rahmenplan für die Ausbildung der Ausbilder und Ausbilderinnen*, BIBB, Bonn., www.bibb.de/dokumente/pdf/HA135.pdf; TA Bildungszentrum (2015[11]), *Ausbildungseignungsprüfung IHK (AEVO).*

Norway: Training for apprentice supervisors is optional, free to participants, and delivered by counties, schools or training offices (owned by companies). Counties provide the course, learning materials, subsistence and travel expenses, while firms pay supervisors during the course. Typically, the training lasts two days (or four half days) per year. Supervisors learn to cover the curriculum, complete evaluation procedures and administrative forms, and prepare and follow through a training plan. The time between training sessions allows supervisors to practice what they have learnt. National guidelines, developed in co-operation with vocational education and training (VET) teacher training institutions, are available on line.

Source: Norwegian Directorate for Education and Training (2009[12]), *Personal Communication* (22 January 2009).

Policy argument 2: With care, learning can be integrated into productive work, benefitting both employers and apprentices

The mix of apprenticeship tasks typically includes more skilled work and less training as apprentices progress

In schemes where apprentices alternate days spent at school or college and days spent in a firm, the mix of tasks gradually evolves to include less training and more productive work (see Figure 5.1 for data from Germany and Switzerland). In some apprenticeship schemes, the time mostly dedicated to training and the time mostly spent on productive work are separated into consecutive periods. For example, in Norway, apprentices typically spend two years training in a vocational school and then work for an employer for two years. At the workplace, one year focuses on training activities and one year on productive work.

Figure 5.1. Activities performed by apprentices in the workplace

By year of apprenticeship

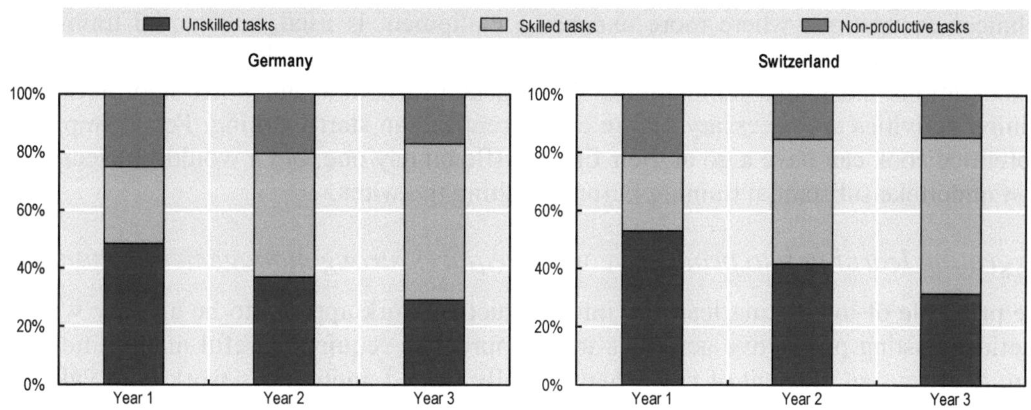

Note: Reference year 2007 for Germany, 2009 for Switzerland.
Source: Adapted from Jansen, A. et al. (2015[13]), "Labour market deregulation and apprenticeship training: A comparison of German and Swiss employers", *European Journal of Industrial Relations*, Vol. 21/4, pp. 353-368, http://dx.doi.org/10.1177/0959680115580687.

StatLink http://dx.doi.org/10.1787/888933828486

Learning can be part of productive or non-productive activities

Many types of learning can take place either through non-productive activities or by being integrated into productive work. For example, after observing their supervisor and receiving instruction, a trainee might practice the targeted skills through simulations (e.g. in a workshop) or by doing real work. Either way, the apprentice gets a chance to practice the task in order to master the skill. However, while undertaking simulations or other exercises apprentices do not produce anything, whereas in a real work environment they can be productive while learning. Apprentices will need more time to complete a given task than an experienced worker and the result might be of lower quality, but they still generate benefits for the firm. Integrating some elements of training into productive activities is therefore, in principle, beneficial from the point of view of firms and neutral from the point of view of apprentices.

There is sometimes room to integrate more learning into productive work

Evidence suggests that with care, learning can often be integrated into productive work, which yields higher benefits for the firm while maintaining learning quality. Research found that in Germany, firms that offer apprenticeships reduced the share of non-productive activities by half between 2000 and 2007, and increased the share of productive work. If firms had just reduced all forms of training, the change would have harmed learning outcomes for apprentices. Instead, data suggest that apprentices continued to spend the same amount of time with instructors as before, firms maintained their level of spending on apprenticeships, and apprentices' productivity compared to skilled workers did not suffer (Jansen et al., 2015[13]). In summary, careful organisation of the time spent in the workplace allowed firms to increase the benefits reaped during the apprenticeship scheme itself, without damaging learning among apprentices.

The scope for learning through productive work varies across occupations

The ease of learning through productive work depends on the occupation: in highly technical occupations where more expensive equipment is used, substantial training is often needed before apprentices can start productive work. In others, health and safety considerations mean that simulations, theoretical instruction and other non-productive training activities are necessary before an apprentice can start working. For example, an apprentice cook can have a go at their first soufflé on day one, but a would-be electrician must undertake substantial training before touching the wires.

Integrating learning into productive work requires strong management capacity

The principle of integrating learning into productive work appears to be an easy win. In practice, trusting productive activities to an apprentice requires careful management, as there is always an element of risk when partially skilled apprentices work with valuable equipment or interact with valued clients. Careful management and training skills are necessary to help a young apprentice, for example, get the soufflé right and avoid the risk of exposing valued customers to soggy scrambled eggs. The implication is that policy tools that improve training capacity in workplaces (as discussed above) can yield benefits to both employers and apprentices: employers can achieve a better financial balance by teaching the same skills as before, but integrating them better into the production process, and apprentices benefit from a consistently strong learning experience.

Apprenticeship assessments must be rigorous

When an employer takes on an apprentice, it commits to develop the skillset targeted by the programme. Employers have some degree of autonomy over how they organise their apprentice's time on the job, as long as they cover that skillset. This autonomy needs to be balanced by rigorous assessments to check that all apprentices have developed the desired skills by the end of the programme.

One challenge is that occupations targeted by apprenticeships require a wide range of skills, including practical technical skills, which are often expensive to test directly, and soft skills (e.g. how to deal with an awkward client), for which traditional paper and pencil tests are poorly adapted. As a result, these aspects of the targeted skillset are often inappropriately assessed in examinations.

- Standards and procedures for assessment should be established to support clear and reliable qualifications. These should cover issues such as what skills are assessed, how the assessment is conducted, and who will carry out the assessment. Mechanisms are necessary to ensure consistency in standards and in the use of the assessment in different parts of a country and at different points of time.
- In light of the wide range of skills required by many occupations targeted by apprenticeships, assessments should incorporate, whenever possible, tests of the full range of skills required in the target occupation. These should include skills not adequately measured by traditional written and oral assessments, including practical technical skills and soft skills.

Policy argument 1: Strong final examinations ensure credible qualifications, while allowing flexibility in how skills are developed

Rigorous final examinations are needed to underpin high-quality apprenticeships

Regarding the on-the-job component of apprenticeships, regulations typically include some requirements regarding the quality of input (e.g. supervisor qualifications, training plan). At the same time, and for good reason, employers typically have considerable autonomy in defining the tasks that apprentices perform on the job. This allows them to adapt the training to the context of the workplace (e.g. staffing arrangements, way of organising production), enabling optimal means of integrating apprentices into their daily activities. Counterbalancing this autonomy, valid and reliable assessments are needed to check whether the apprentice is effectively learning on the job. Final examinations, which verify if the apprentice has acquired the full targeted skillset at the end of the programme, are particularly important.

Rigorous assessments can also benefit those who acquire skills through different pathways

Reliable assessments are also needed to implement the tools discussed in Chapter 4: the possibility for individuals who already have some of the relevant skills to complete an apprenticeship faster than the standard duration, and the option of taking the final apprentice examination without pursuing the full apprenticeship programme itself. These options involve non-standard routes to skills, with either an adjusted training programme or no mandatory training programme at all. When a qualification is delivered with limited or no programmatic requirements, its value in the labour market will depend on the credibility of the underlying assessments.

Policy argument 2: Assessments need to test the range of skills required by the target occupation

Technical skills are often inappropriately assessed because of the costs involved

Some technical skills can be adequately assessed through paper and pencil examinations (e.g. when the focus is on theoretical knowledge), however, such tools are poorly adapted for the assessment of practical technical skills. Direct assessments of practical technical skills in an authentic working environment can be very costly because of the material and equipment involved. As a result, there can be a temptation to skimp on the assessment of some of these skills.

Technology can reduce the costs of assessment

Technology might create new and cheaper ways of assessing practical skills. For example, the skills of a would-be CNC (Computer Numerical Control) technician might be tested on a CNC simulator, avoiding the high costs of using a real machine and materials. A recent research initiative in Germany developed technology-based tools for the assessment of vocational skills, with encouraging results (see Box 5.2).

Box 5.2. Technology-based assessments in Germany

The ASCOT (Technology-based Assessment of Skills and Competences in Vocational Education and Training) research initiative was launched in 2011, with the aim of developing methods for technology-based final assessments in VET. The initiative included projects with experts in the fields of science and practice in five occupations. Instruments for assessment were developed based on real life situations. For example, apprentices training to be medical assistants were confronted with a virtual doctor's office simulating interactions with patients. The instruments proved highly suitable for the assessment of technical and professional competences, occupation-specific social and communication skills, and occupationally relevant literacy and numeracy skills. They also improved the objectivity of assessments and the test motivation of candidates, and were more efficient than traditional assessment tools. The follow-up initiative, ASCOT+, will aim to transfer the instruments into practice: supporting teaching and learning, as well as informing the development of competence-based training regulations and examinations.

Source: BMBF (2018[14]), *Technologiebasierte Kompetenzmessung in der beruflichen Bildung* (ASCOT), *Ergebnisse und Bedeutung für Politik und Praxis*, www.bmbf.de/pub/ASCOT.pdf.

Social skills are crucial to many jobs, including those requiring a vocational qualification. Traditionally the focus of vocational (and indeed academic) examinations has been on theoretical knowledge and technical skills, with little or no attention given to social skills. One reason for this is that social skills are hard to test with traditional paper and pencil examinations. Designing and implementing assessments that test how good a car mechanic apprentice is at handling awkward clients is much harder than testing their knowledge of mechatronics. However, socio-emotional skills might carry more weight in the skillsets required for the vocational occupations of the future, so their assessment is important. Data from the United States show that demand for non-routine interpersonal skills has strongly increased in recent years (Autor and Price, 2013[15]).

There are promising practices in the assessment of occupation-specific socio-emotional skills

There are some promising initiatives in the assessment of occupation-specific socio-emotional skills, and various countries have developed and used assessments that focus on social skills, for example through role-playing. In Switzerland, real estate agents aiming to pass the professional examination for property managers must pass an oral examination, where they might, for example, be required to negotiate with an elderly couple regarding their poorly kept building (see Box 5.3).

Box 5.3. Oral examination for property managers in Switzerland

Candidates for the professional examination in property management must pass, among others, an oral examination focusing mostly on social and "methodological" competences. The examination includes a role-playing scenario, with examiners playing the role of clients.

An example of a role-playing scenario

The candidate is meeting the retired owners of a building who wish to delegate property management to an agency. The building has various problems (e.g. rusty swings in the playground), so the candidate is expected to make proposals for renovation and taking care of the building, as well as advise about the transferal of ownership to the owners' children while continuing to receive rental income.

Examiners evaluate the candidate following an assessment grid

Social competences include communication skills, behaviour and appearance. To obtain grade 6 in communication, the candidate must express themselves clearly, be an active listener and give focused replies. Methodological competences include integrative thinking, problem solving and negotiation techniques. To obtain grade 6 in negotiation, the candidate must negotiate successfully using plausible arguments. Some aspects of technical knowledge are checked during the discussion, for example, asking the candidate to describe the legal basis concerning subletting the rental property.

Examiners are also observed during the examination

An observer, from the State Secretariat for Education, Research and Innovation checks whether the examiners meet expectations in their role (e.g. clear discussion points, instructions and roles). Their performance is rated as very good, satisfactory, or not satisfactory. Following the examination, the observer gives feedback to the examiners. This element is particularly important if the candidate appeals to challenge the examination result.

Source: Kis, V. and H. Windisch (2018[16]), "Making skills transparent: Recognising vocational skills acquired through work-based learning", *OECD Education Working Papers*, No. 180, https://doi.org/10.1787/5830c400-en.

Entrepreneurial skills also need adequate attention

High-level vocational qualifications, for example in many professional and master craftsman qualifications, often aim to prepare people to run their own business. Some examination procedures also include an assessment of entrepreneurship skills. In Germany, master craftsperson examinations were revised in 2001 to increase the attention paid to the skills needed to run a business, not only at present, but also in response to changing workplace requirements (see Box 5.4).

Box 5.4. Reformed master craftsperson examinations in Germany

Since 2001, revisions of master craftsperson examinations in various occupations have increased emphasis on candidates' capacity to run their own business, train apprentices, and adapt to changing workplace requirements.

Part I of the assessment now comprises a technical exam, a related expert discussion, and an optional situation-specific task. Candidates choose the focus of their craftsperson exam project themselves. The examination commission devises the project assignment, leaving room for suggestions from the examinees. The project resembles a customer order, and encompasses planning, implementation and documentation and an expert discussion with the examination board. Situation-specific tasks are used to check the candidates' skills in areas not covered by the project work.

Part II of the assessment now requires the examinees to prove their capacity to identify, analyse and solve work-related problems. The new structure is even more oriented towards workplace requirements and includes components on trade-specific technical skills, order processing, business management and business organisation. In each of these components, at least one case study must be included.

Source: ZWH (n.d.[17]), *Geänderte Anforderungen in der Meisterprüfung im Handwerk*, Zentralstelle fur die Weiterbildung im Handwerk e.V (ZWH), www.q-zwh.de/pruefer/index.php?id=42&tx_ttnews[tt_news]=23&tx_ttnews[backPid]=28&cHash=f19ae37d9e.

Training for assessors can help ensure valid and reliable assessments

In some countries, training for assessors in vocational examinations is mandatory to ensure the consistency of assessment methods across regions, firms or training institutions. In Switzerland, most assessors in apprenticeship examinations must complete targeted training and receive federal certification (Felser, 2016[18]). In Norway, assessors in apprenticeship examinations must attend training offered by the regional education authorities, receive mentoring support, and can pursue professional development courses set up in co-operation with higher education institutions (Ure, 2015[19]). In Austria and Germany, training for assessors is optional (see Box 5.5).

Box 5.5. Training for assessors of apprentices

Austria

At the end of apprenticeships, members of the examination commission can become a certified assessor after attending a one-day programme composed of at least eight 50-minute modules. Regional apprenticeship offices offer the training, which covers the examination procedure, the distribution of roles, examination simulations, performance evaluation, as well as issues such as how to handle nervous candidates and how to give feedback.

Source: ibw (2016[20]), *Zertifizierte/r Prüfer/in für Lehrabschlussprüfungen*, www.qualitaet-lehre.at/lehrabschlusspruefung/infos-fuer-prueferinnen/zertifizierter-prueferin-fuer-lehrabschlusspruefungen/.

Germany

The preparation of assessors may involve an exchange of experience, the consultation of relevant regulations, preparatory seminars and exam shadowing. The vast majority of assessors have been found by survey to agree that exchanging experience is the best way to learn. Assessor days are organised by chambers of commerce and offer a platform for such exchanges. The Federal Institute for VET (BIBB) provides an online platform that allows assessors to access up-to-date information on training seminars and exchange experience.

Source: Prüferportal (2016[21]), "Prüfung", www.prueferportal.org/html/719.php; Prüfer portal (2016[22]), "Prüferin werden", www.prueferportal.org/html/146.php; Prüferportal (2016[23]), *Meisterprüfungsausschüsse*, www.prueferportal.org/html/1546.php.

Conclusion

This chapter explores how governments and employers can ensure the best possible learning experiences for apprentices whilst in the workplace, and draws on international evidence to highlight the critical importance of such on-the-job training. Effective practice seeks to build training into as much of an apprentice's time at work as is reasonable. It cannot be taken for granted that employers will have the capacity to train well. Governments and social partners can require, or encourage, apprentice supervisors to undertake training themselves and help managers to design work practices to maximise apprentice learning within productive work, as is suitable to different apprenticeships. Rigorous assessment, overseen by appropriate training examiners, is an essential characteristic of strong apprenticeship systems. Final examinations should not only test theoretical and technical knowledge and skills, but also address the fuller demands of the associated occupation, such as personal interaction or social skills. Simulations and role-playing exercises with examiners are innovative means of testing the full range of knowledge and skills demanded by an apprenticeship.

References

Autor, D. and B. Price (2013), *The Changing Task Composition of the US Labor Market: An Update of Autor, Levy, and Murnane (2003)*, https://economics.mit.edu/files/11600. [15]

BIBB (2009), "Ausbilder-Eignungsverordnung Vom 21 Januar 2009", *Bundesgesetzblatt* 5, http://www.bibb.de/dokumente/pdf/ausbilder_eignungsverordnung.pdf. [10]

BIBB (2009), *Empfehlung des Hauptausschusses des Bundesinstituts für Berufsbildung zum Rahmenplan für die Ausbildung der Ausbilder und Ausbilderinnen*, (Recommendation of the Main Committee of the Federal Institute for Vocational Education and Training on the Framework for the Training of Trainers), Federal Institute for Vocational Education and Training (BIBB) , Bonn, https://www.bibb.de/dokumente/pdf/HA135.pdf. [5]

BMBF (2018), *Technologiebasierte Kompetenzmessung in der beruflichen Bildung (ASCOT), Ergebnisse und Bedeutung für Politik und Praxis*, (Technology-based Competence Measurement in Vocational Education and Training (ASCOT), Results and Significance for Politics and Practice), BMBF, Bonn, https://www.bmbf.de/pub/ASCOT.pdf. [14]

Felser, R. (2016), *SFIVET – Swiss Federal Institute for Vocational Education and Training*. [18]

Government of Ontario (2017), *Hire an Apprentice*, http://www.ontario.ca/page/hire-apprentice (accessed on 1 August 2017). [8]

ibw (2016), *Zertifizierte/r Prüfer/in für Lehrabschlussprüfungen*, Institut für Bildungsforschung der Wirtschaft, Wien, https://www.qualitaet-lehre.at/lehrabschlusspruefung/infos-fuer-prueferinnen/zertifizierter-prueferin-fuer-lehrabschlusspruefungen/ (accessed on 28 June 2016). [20]

Industry Training Authority (2017), *Apprenticeships Who's Who*, http://www.itabc.ca/about-apprentices/apprenticeship-who%E2%80%99s-who (accessed on 1 August 2017). [9]

Jansen, A. et al. (2015), "Labour market deregulation and apprenticeship training: A comparison of German and Swiss employers", *European Journal of Industrial Relations*, Vol. 21/4, pp. 353-368, http://dx.doi.org/10.1177/0959680115580687. [13]

Kis, V. and H. Windisch (2018), "Making skills transparent: Recognising vocational skills acquired through workbased learning", *OECD Education Working Papers*, No. 180, OECD Publishing, Paris, http://dx.doi.org/10.1787/5830c400-en. [16]

Kuczera, M. (2017), "Striking the right balance: Costs and benefits of apprenticeship", *OECD Education Working Papers*, No. 153, OECD Publishing, Paris, http://dx.doi.org/10.1787/995fff01-en. [1]

Kuczera, M., T. Bastianić and S. Field (2018), *Apprenticeship and Vocational Education and Training in Israel*, OECD Reviews of Vocational Education and Training, OECD Publishing, Paris, https://doi.org/10.1787/9789264302051-en. [7]

Kuczera, M. and S. Field (2018), *Apprenticeship in England, United Kingdom*, OECD Reviews of Vocational Education and Training, OECD Publishing, Paris, http://dx.doi.org/10.1787/9789264298507-en. [4]

Mühlemann, S. (2016), "The cost and benefits of work-based learning", *OECD Education Working Papers*, No. 143, OECD Publishing, Paris, https://doi.org/10.1787/5jlpl4s6g0zv-en. [3]

Norwegian Directorate for Education and Training (2009), *Personal Communication (22 January 2009)*. [12]

Prüferporta (2016), *Meisterprüfungsausschüsse*, http://www.prueferportal.org/html/1546.php (accessed on 23 May 2016). [23]

Prüferportal (2016), *Die Zusammensetzung des Prüfungsausschusses*, http://www.prueferportal.org/html/719.php (accessed on 23 May 2016). [21]

Prüferportal (2016), *Prüfer/in werden*, http://www.prueferportal.org/html/146.php (accessed on 1 June 2016). [22]

Queensland Government (2018), *The Employer Resource Assessment and Training Plan - Expectations of the Department*, https://training.qld.gov.au/apprenticeshipsinfo/information-resources/employer-capacity (accessed on 20 July 2018). [6]

TA Bildungszentrum (2015), *Ausbildungseignungsprüfung IHK (AEVO)*, https://www.ta.de/ausbildereignungspruefung-ihk-aevo.html. [11]

Ure, O. (2015), *How Informal and Non-formal Learning is Recognised in Europe. Norway Country Report*, Bertelsmann Stiftung, Gütersloh, https://www.bertelsmann-stiftung.de/en/publications/publication/did/norway-country-report-how-informal-and-non-formal-learning-is-recognised-in-europe/ (accessed on 23 April 2018). [19]

Wolter, S. and P. Ryan (2011), "Apprenticeship", in *Handbook of the Economics of Education*, Elsevier, https://ideas.repec.org/h/eee/educhp/3-11.html. [2]

ZWH (n.d.), *Geänderte Anforderungen in der Meisterprüfung im Handwerk*, Zentralstelle fur die Weiterbildung im Handwerk e.V (ZHW), http://www.q-zwh.de/pruefer/index.php?id=42&tx_ttnews[tt_news]=23&tx_ttnews[backPid]=28&cHash=f19ae37d9e. [17]

Chapter 6. How to make apprenticeships work for youth at risk?

This chapter focuses on youth at risk: young people who are unemployed (often called NEET or not in education employment or training) or at risk of such an outcome. It identifies some of the common additional barriers facing such youth, including: weaker literacy, numeracy and general education; lack of work experience; and lack of relevant social networks and soft skills. The chapter critically reviews a number of policy interventions that might serve to increase the likelihood of employers offering apprenticeships to youth at risk, including financial subsidies, apprenticeship duration, preparatory programmes, and personalised support over the programme of training.

The statistical data for Israel are supplied by and under the responsibility of the relevant Israeli authorities. The use of such data by the OECD is without prejudice to the status of the Golan Heights, East Jerusalem and Israeli settlements in the West Bank under the terms of international law.

Issues and challenges

Apprenticeships can improve the job and life prospects of youth at risk

Apprenticeships have attracted increasing attention as a tool to support effective school-to-work transition, and can help to tackle youth unemployment and inactivity. The benefits of apprenticeships are especially significant for youth at risk, who are most likely to struggle to complete school or find good jobs. In this chapter, youth at risk are defined as youth not in employment, education or training (NEET), and those at risk of becoming NEET. International evidence suggests that apprenticeships may help school-to-work transition: OECD countries with a high share of youth in apprenticeships have lower rates of youth struggling to transition to employment (Quintini and Martin, 2014[1]). In the United States, a review of programme evaluations showed that combining vocational training with work placements can improve labour market outcomes for young people (Sattar, 2010[2]). The benefits of such programmes are sometimes not job-related: programmes involving work placements can help by keeping young people out of trouble and by reducing arrest, incarceration and mortality rates (Gelber, Isen and Kessler, 2014[3]; Sattar, 2010[2]).

Youth at risk are likely to face more challenges to find a placement

For youth at risk, however, finding a good apprenticeship can be difficult. Those living in underprivileged areas often have fewer job opportunities, and family and friends may be jobless or in low skill jobs, limiting the scope for informal connections to employers and recruiters. Even if contacts could be built with employers taking apprentices, one major hurdle remains: ensuring that employers actually offer apprenticeship placements to youth at risk.

The potential of apprenticeships will be realised only if they align with business interests

Some firms may take on young people at risk as apprentices through a desire to help or foster social cohesion in the community. However, employers also need to run a business and make a profit, and few can afford to hire an apprentice if that would generate losses for their enterprise. If the potential of apprenticeships for youth at risk is to be fully realised, programmes must not only provide an opportunity for employers to show social responsibility, but must also be well aligned with their business objectives. This requires a good understanding of the financial implications for employers of taking on youth at risk as apprentices.

One challenge is that youth at risk tend to have weaker skills than their peers

Youth at risk usually have relatively weak skills, which is one reason why employers may be reluctant to take them on as apprentices. Some of these weaknesses will be academic: NEETs tend to have weaker literacy and numeracy skills than young people in education, employment or training (Figure 6.1) Sometimes, the weakness concerns soft skills and personality attributes: studies have found that high school dropouts in the United States, and those who dropped out but completed high school through a second chance programme, had weaker non-cognitive or soft skills in some areas (e.g. persistence and conscientiousness) than those who never dropped out (Heckman and Rubinstein, 2001[4]; Heckman, Stixrud and Urzua, 2006[5]). Such differences between the typical profile of youth at risk and their peers are important for employers, because the skills of apprentices will affect how they perform at work and whether they will be able to successfully complete their training.

Figure 6.1. NEETs face more difficulties with basic skills

Percentage of adults aged 16-29 with weak literacy or numeracy skills

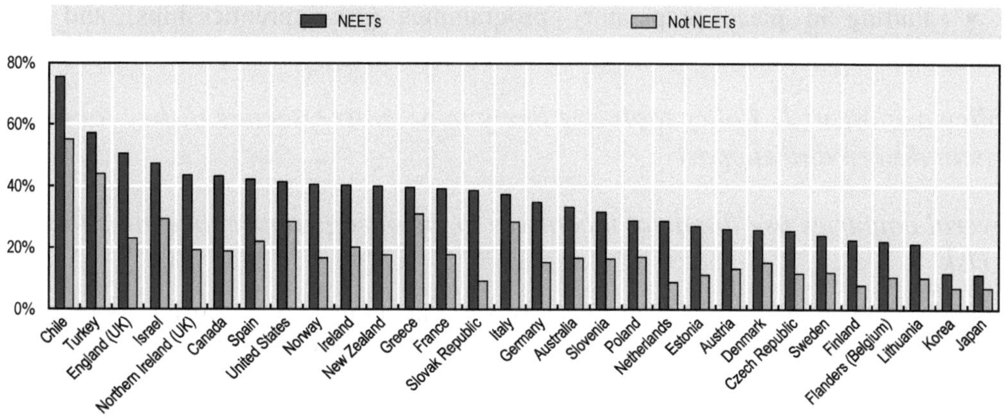

Note: Weak literacy or numeracy skills are defined as below Level 2.
Source: OECD (2015[6]), OECD Survey of Adult Skills (PIAAC) (Database 2012, 2015), www.oecd.org/site/piaac/publicdataandanalysis.htm.

StatLink http://dx.doi.org/10.1787/888933828505

Taking on a young person at risk as an apprentice is costlier for employers

Weaker basic skills make apprentices less productive at work – an apprentice in car mechatronics will contribute less to business in a garage if they struggle to browse the vehicle manufacturer's technical portal. Gaps in soft skills have a similar effect – some apprentices may struggle to arrive on time or handle conflicts with colleagues. Filling those gaps is one of the objectives of an apprenticeship, but it requires time and support, and some will need to catch up with initial weaknesses and may progress more slowly than average. This means that many youth at risk in apprenticeships will need more help to develop the required skills. The implication for firms is fewer benefits through productive work and higher costs in terms of instruction time.

Apprenticeship schemes need to be designed in ways that address the needs of youth at risk, while remaining attractive to employers

To realise the full potential of apprenticeships for youth at risk, it is important to ensure that the prospect of taking on a young person at risk aligns with the business interests of enterprises. This requires shifting the balance of costs and benefits to employers to make it more attractive for them to offer opportunities to this group. International evidence suggests that this is best done through non-financial measures.

Changing the parameters of apprenticeship schemes (e.g. apprentice wages, duration and how apprentices' time is spent) can help make apprenticeships for youth at risk more attractive to employers. This may be implemented by:

- Creating a targeted apprenticeship scheme with a modified design that is suitable to the specific needs of youth at risk and is attractive to employers, such as a shorter programme.
- Putting in place preparatory programmes (pre-apprenticeships) and support measures for youth at risk enrolled on regular apprenticeship schemes.

Policy argument 1: Policy tools are likely to be most effective if they focus on system design and support

Several countries use financial incentives to encourage apprenticeships for youth at risk

Several countries use subsidies or tax breaks to encourage firms to offer apprenticeships to young people who struggle to find a placement. In Austria, firms taking on young people in "integrative apprenticeships" (IBA) receive higher subsidies than other firms, and public resources cover some of the additional training needed by apprentices and trainers in the firm (Wirtschaftskammer Österreich (WKO), 2016[7]). Australia offers a subsidy to those engaging an apprentice from specific groups, such as indigenous Australians and job seekers with severe barriers to employment (Australian Government, 2017[8]). France offers a higher tax break to firms that take on disadvantaged apprentices, including young people without a qualification and youth who have signed a "voluntary integration contract", which targets those most disconnected from employment (Service-Public-Pro, 2016[9]).

Effectively targeting youth at risk is challenging

As set out in Chapter 2, international evidence offers limited support in favour of financial incentives as a means of encouraging apprenticeship provision. The arguments against subsidies to support youth at risk in apprenticeships are similar. Typically, there are sectors of the economy with labour shortages where employers are very happy to take on youth at risk as apprentices. Such sectors are likely to take advantage of any subsidy available, but it will mostly be deadweight with few additional apprentices being taken on. The evaluation of such a targeted subsidy by Germany illustrates this point. Germany launched a bonus scheme in 2008 that rewarded firms offering an apprenticeship to youth who had failed to find a placement or possessed only lower secondary schooling or less. Despite efforts to reward only additional placements (e.g. the bonus was offered only if the firm offered more placements than they had over the preceding three years), the evaluation of the scheme found that it made a difference to only one in ten cases – the other apprentices would have been hired anyway (Bonin, 2013[10]). The scheme was scrapped in 2010. The amount offered seemed too low to make a difference, and even with the bonus firms faced net costs by the end of the apprenticeship, even more so as disadvantaged participants needed more instruction time. This meant that firms ended up offering placements to young people they intended to hire upon completion, and who, – but in the vast majority of cases, would have been offered a place even without the subsidy (Mühlemann, 2016[11]).

Policy efforts are best focused on measures that do not involve financial incentives

International experience suggests that it is better to focus on tools that make offering apprenticeships to youth at risk attractive to employers, but without giving them money directly. For example, the evaluation of the German bonus scheme found that firms thought that strengthening basic skills among applicants and offering more support to weaker apprentices during training would have been more helpful than a subsidy (Wenzelmann, 2016[12]). Research from Switzerland (Mühlemann, Braendli and Wolter, 2013[13]) suggests that firms are willing to invest extra instruction time in apprentices with poor school grades, at least in occupations where they expect to reap net benefits during the course of the apprenticeship. This suggests that designing programmes in a way that allows firms to at least break even by the end of the training period is important to ensure access to apprenticeships among youth at risk.

Policy argument 2: Programmes can be designed to work for both employers and youth at risk

It is possible to design a programme for youth at risk that also works for employers and apprentices

Research evidence shows that by carefully adjusting the parameters of apprenticeship schemes (e.g. duration, apprentice wage, balance of time spent with the firms vs. at school or college), it is possible to design schemes that work for both youth at risk and employers. Employers need to break even by the end of the apprenticeship, while youth at risk need to develop targeted skills. For example, in Switzerland, firms that offer two-year apprenticeships designed with youth at risk explicitly in mind break even, on average, by the end of the training period. This is achieved while delivering good training: nearly half of completers proceed to higher level apprenticeships, and three-quarters of the remaining half find a job upon completion (Fuhrer and Schweri, 2010[14]). The programme includes various support tools (see Box 6.2).

Shorter programmes with flexible duration may work better for youth at risk

Offering apprenticeships in occupations for which a relatively short duration is suitable may help achieve higher completion rates. In Switzerland, two-year apprenticeships were created for youth at risk (most apprenticeships last three or four years). Austria has a special "integrative apprenticeship" in which apprentices may obtain a partial qualification or take longer to complete than an average apprentice (BMWFW, 2016[15]). As for any apprenticeship, programmes must not become dead ends: upon completion, apprentices should have the possibility to progress to higher levels of training.

Some occupations may fit youth at risk better than others

Employers may be more ready to go the extra mile and help struggling apprentices when they need those apprentices to contribute to production, rather than be left with training costs and few productive benefits. Research has found that in occupations where Swiss firms expected to break even by the end of apprenticeship, more attention was given to apprentices with poor school grades to help them catch up. The opposite occurred in occupations where firms hired apprentices to recruit the best upon completion. In these cases it was the highest performers who received extra training (Mühlemann, Braendli and Wolter, 2013[13]), which is not surprising, as if the key benefit for the firm comes from recruiting the best, they will focus on making the best apprentices even better. The implication is that occupations where firms can obtain benefits during the training period may work better for youth who need extra support. When employers hire apprentices with a view to reap benefits from productive work, rather than the prospect of recruiting them, it is particularly important to ensure that apprentices also learn useful occupational skills and are not exploited as cheap labour – Chapter 5 focuses on this issue.

Box 6.1. Apprenticeship schemes designed to serve youth at risk

Two-year apprenticeships (EBA) in Switzerland

These programmes target young people aged 15 and above who have completed lower secondary education, are at risk of dropping out from education and training, or who struggle to find a three or four-year apprenticeship. They are offered in around 60 occupations, such as retail sales assistant, healthcare assistant and hairdresser (SDBB, 2016[16]). Their structure is similar to longer apprenticeships and they combine firm-based and school-based components. EBA apprentices benefit from support measures, such as individual tutoring, remedial courses and support from in-company supervisors (SBFI, 2014[17]).

Those who complete may progress to three or four-year apprenticeships, typically joining the second year of the programme – 41% do so within two years of completion. Among those who do not pursue further training, 75% find employment within six months of completion (SBFI, 2014[17]).

Source: Fuhrer, M., and J. Schweri (2010[14]) "Two-year apprenticeships for young people with learning difficulties: a cost-benefit analysis for training firms", *Empirical Research in Vocational Education and Training,* Vol. 2/22, www.skbf-csre.ch; SBFI (2014[17]), *Zweijährige Berufliche Grundbildung mit Eidgenössischem Berufsattest*, Staatssekretariat für Bildung, Forschung und Innovation, www.sbfi.admin.ch/berufsbildung; SDBB (2016[16]), Career guidance website "EBA-Beruf – 2-jährige Lehre", www.berufsberatung.ch.

Integrative apprenticeships (IBA) in Austria

Integrative apprenticeships were introduced in 2003 and accounted for 6% of apprentices in 2014 (Dornmayr, 2012[18]). They target learners with special needs, people with disabilities, and those without a basic school-leaving certificate (BMWFW, 2016[15]). Participants can take longer to complete by one or two years, or may obtain a partial qualification. They receive support both during work placement and at school. The school-based component is adapted to the needs of IBA apprentices: teachers can attend targeted training courses, additional assistance is available to support teaching, and class sizes are reduced. Those in the partial qualification pathway follow individualised curricula and attend smaller classes.

Source: BMWFW (2016[15]), *Lehrausbildung in verlängerter Lehrzeit und in Teilqualifikation*, www.bmwfw.gv.at/Berufsausbildung; Dornmayr, H. (2012[18]), *Berufseinmündung von AbsolventInnen der Integrativen Berufsausbildung*, Institut für Bildungsforschung der Wirtschaft, www.bmwfw.gv.at/Berufsausbildung/LehrlingsUndBerufsausbildung.

Youth at risk often need preparatory programmes to get them ready for apprenticeships

When apprentices are well prepared – for example, they have caught up with any gaps in literacy or numeracy, have carefully chosen their target occupation, and are ready to operate and learn in a real work environment – they will be more attractive in the eyes of potential employers and have better chances of completing their training. Many countries pursue extensive pre-apprenticeship programmes to this end.

- Pre-apprenticeship programmes encourage and offer financial resources to prepare youth at risk for apprenticeships.
- Given the diversity of approaches in this area, and the limited evidence base, new initiatives should be piloted and evaluated with the most effective programmes rolled out.

Policy argument 1: Pre-apprenticeship programmes can help transition youth at risk into apprenticeships

Pre-apprenticeships can help prepare youth at risk for an apprenticeship programme

Given the many challenges of encouraging employers to offer apprenticeships to young people who are inadequately prepared, an alternative approach is to tackle weaknesses in the skillset of youth at risk before the apprenticeship starts. The objective is to help young people at risk with some of their foundation skills in such a way as to improve their chances of finding a good apprenticeship placement. Such pre-apprenticeships can address weaknesses in literacy or numeracy, develop initial vocational skills, and improve key soft and employability skills. Employers will find better prepared potential apprentices a more worthwhile investment as they will contribute more easily to production, learn faster, need less support to remedy initial weaknesses, and will be less likely to drop out.

Their role is particularly important when an apprenticeship is a pathway within upper secondary vocational education and training (VET)

Pre-apprenticeship programmes, which build a bridge to apprenticeships, are found in many OECD countries (see Table 6.1). In addition to developing academic, vocational and soft skills, programmes often aim to help match participants to available placements by offering career guidance, work placements and job search training. In countries where upper secondary VET is usually delivered through youth apprenticeships (e.g. several countries in continental Europe), failure to find a placement may lead to disconnection from the labour market and learning opportunities. In these countries, pre-apprenticeships act as a bridge between lower secondary and upper secondary education. Sometimes, programmes target youth at risk without links to formal pre-apprenticeship frameworks. For example, in the United States, many programmes are developed by public and private stakeholders, which creates both a rich field of innovation and a challenge for sustaining and upscaling approaches that work.

Table 6.1. Pre-apprenticeship programmes in selected OECD countries

Country	Programme	Target group	Typical duration	Content
Australia	Pre-apprenticeship		6-12 months	General employability skills, occupation-specific skills.
England (United Kingdom)	Traineeship	Youth aged 16-24 qualified below level 3 with little work experience and not in employment	6 weeks-6 months	Work experience placement, work preparation training, literacy and mathematics if needed.
Germany	Introductory training (EQ)	Youth aged 16-25	6-12 months	Work-based learning, optional school-based component.
	Preparatory VET year	Youth aged below 18	12 months (extension up to 18 months)	General subjects at vocational school. Exploration of three occupational fields (including work placements).
	Basic vocational year		12 months	Vocational theory and practice in a selected field. Work placement.
Scotland (United Kingdom)	Certificate of Work Readiness	16-24 year-olds	10-12 weeks	Off-the-job training targeting employability skills. Work experience.
Switzerland	SEMO	Youth aged less than 25	6 months (extension up to 9.5 months)	1-2 days a week at a vocational school.
	Bridging measures		12 months	Literacy, mathematics, motivation and career guidance.
United States	Pre-apprenticeship			Literacy, mathematics, work-readiness training.

Note: Additionally, pre-apprenticeship programmes are in the process of being introduced in Canada.
Source: Kis, V. (2016[19]), "Work-based learning for youth at risk: Getting employers on board", *OECD Education Working Papers*, No. 150, http://dx.doi.org/10.1787/5e122a91-en.

Policy argument 2: Programmes that allow learners to start apprenticeships outside firms should focus on transition into the regular system

Some countries have programmes that allow young people to start an apprenticeship outside firms

A different approach is to allow young people to start a form of "shadow" apprenticeship without a work placement, and then help them transition into a regular apprenticeship. For example, Austria established special courses (called *überbetriebliche Ausbildung* [ÜBA]) for young people who cannot find a placement, which provide a shadow apprenticeship based in a workshop that simulates the employer. Around a quarter of participants transition into regular apprenticeships, the remainder obtain the same qualification as apprentices but through a school-based programme (Hofbauer, Kugi-Mazza and Sinowatz, 2014[20]). In Germany, similar programmes (*Berufsausbildung in außerbetrieblichen Einrichtungen* [BaE]) are offered in several occupations and target disadvantaged youth and those with learning difficulties. After the first year, participants are encouraged to find a regular apprentice position, and those who do not succeed may continue within the programme and obtain a qualification (Bonin et al., 2010[21]).

However, such programmes miss some important benefits of apprenticeships

Such programmes have advantages for young people who cannot immediately find a regular apprenticeship placement as they can start earning a wage and obtain a qualification. However, these programmes lack some of the benefits of regular apprenticeships, for example, participants do not have the same opportunities to develop soft skills as regular apprentices (e.g. they do not interact with real bosses and colleagues). Also, the supply of apprenticeship positions in firms sends a signal about their needs – in these programmes those signals are missed.

Policy argument 3: Given the wide range of approaches in this area, more evaluation evidence would be desirable

Evaluations are essential to identify what works

Pre-apprenticeship programmes tend to be costly, so identifying which approaches work best is essential. If a pre-apprenticeship programme does not develop useful skills it risks becoming stigmatising for participants rather than a pathway to good jobs. Evaluation evidence can help to identify whether a programme works so that successful initiatives can be expanded and unsuccessful ones discontinued.

Obtaining solid evidence is difficult

Even within individual countries, programmes offered often vary in terms of content, duration and funding, so average results may be a poor indicator of the quality of individual programmes. In addition, identifying what would have happened to participants had they not pursued the programme is a challenge. In most countries, all eligible youth willing to enter are provided with access, so a comparison of those offered the programmes and those not offered the programme is not possible. Pre-apprenticeship participants tend to be more disadvantaged and have weaker skills than those who choose other pathways or jobs at the same age (Autorengruppe Bildungsberichterstattung, 2016[22]; Karmel and Oliver, 2011[23]). This means that higher dropout rates from apprenticeships among those who pursued a pre-apprenticeship (as found in Germany) may reflect weaker skills at the outset, rather than the poor quality of pre-apprenticeship programmes. In Australia, evaluations found that the link between pre-apprenticeship participation and apprenticeship completion varied across trades (Karmel and Oliver, 2011[23]).

Youth at risk often require additional support over the duration of the apprenticeship

Youth at risk are more likely to struggle to complete their apprenticeship than an average apprentice, and dropout commonly leads to weak labour market outcomes. It is also costly for employers, who will have invested in finding and training the apprentice and, following a dropout, are left with costs and no chance of benefitting from apprentices' contributions to productive work.

The difficulties faced by youth at risk during apprenticeships may concern academic coursework, conflict with the training company, or may be of personal nature. To increase the chances of successful completion and help apprentices participate in the training firm's activities:

- Youth at risk who undertake apprenticeships should be provided with additional support. This may include remedial courses (e.g. in literacy and numeracy), mentoring and coaching.
- Employers should be helped to build their capacity to provide apprenticeships to youth at risk. For example, support with how to handle difficulties that may arise with apprentices, and how to deliver training effectively on-the-job (e.g. training for supervisors, online forum for supervisors).

Policy argument 1: Supporting youth at risk during apprentices can benefit both employers and apprentices

Once access to apprenticeship is secured, support is needed to avoid dropout

Many young people at risk find completing an apprenticeship challenging. Data from England (United Kingdom), Germany and Switzerland show that apprentices with a minority background, weak school results and learning difficulties, have higher dropout rates. Soft skills and apprentice motivation are also important, with employers reporting a lack of effort as a common cause for dropout (Gambin and Hogarth, 2016[24]; Autorengruppe Bildungsberichterstattung, 2016[22]; Stalder and Schmid, 2006[25]). Supporting apprentices during their training can help them achieve a qualification, while also benefitting their employers.

Support during apprenticeships benefits employers, which encourages them to offer placements

Youth at risk tend to need more instruction time (creating higher costs for employers), will develop skills more slowly (generating fewer benefits for the firm), and are more likely to drop out. Offering extra support helps apprentices to learn faster and overcome any difficulties, get on better with their employer and school, and have better chances of completion. As a result, employers benefit from better performing apprentices and can reduce the risks of costly dropout. The availability of additional support can encourage employers to hire youth at risk as apprentices. For example, a master carpenter may be reluctant to take on a young person who struggled at school as they may worry about the apprentice not being able to cope with the mathematics needed to work out the rise and run for a staircase. If extra support is available, this may reassure the master carpenter that the apprentice will fit in with the firm.

Schools and mentors can help overcome learning and personal problems

Apprentices may receive help with academic or technical coursework (e.g. remedial courses) or with preparing for exams. Mentors or coaches may help apprentices with everyday problems and act as mediators if problems arise between the apprentice and their firm or school.

Box 6.2. State-funded apprenticeship assistance

Australia

The Apprenticeship Support Network aims to help employers to recruit, train and retain apprentices, and to help apprentices to succeed. Eleven regional networks provide advice and support services for employers and apprentices through universal services for all employers and apprentices, administrative support, payment processing and regular contact, as well as targeted services for those needing additional support. Where there is a risk of non-completion, additional services (e.g. mentoring) will help apprentices and employers to work through difficulties. Those who may be unsuited to an apprenticeship will receive help to find alternative training pathways. Services provided by the Network are funded by the Australian Government and delivered by private providers.

Austria

Training assistants, funded by public resources, work extensively with youth in integrative apprenticeships, which target youth with special needs, disabilities and dropouts from basic schooling. They take care of administrative tasks and prepare the firm for the arrival of the apprentice. During the training period they provide tutorial support and act as mediators if difficulties arise. Most training assistants are trained in special education and have work experience with disadvantaged youth.

Germany

Apprenticeship assistance, funded by government, is offered free of charge to apprentices or dropouts to help them find a way back into apprenticeships. Assistance includes remedial education and help with homework, mentoring to help with everyday problems, and mediation in case of conflict with the school or company. A support plan is established with the apprentice, which typically involves three hours of individual assistance per week, as well as some group sessions.

Switzerland

Apprentices in two-year programmes are entitled to publicly funded individual coaching. Around half of those entitled take up the opportunity, mostly to tackle weak language skills, learning difficulties or psychological problems. Most coaches are former teachers, learning therapists or social workers, and receive targeted training in preparation for their job (e.g. 300-hour training in Zurich).

Source: Kis, V. (2016[19]), "Work-based learning for youth at risk: Getting employers on board", *OECD Education Working Papers*, No. 150, http://dx.doi.org/10.1787/5e122a91-en; Australian Government (2018[26]), *Australian Apprenticeship Support Network*, www.australianapprenticeships.gov.au/australian-apprenticeship-support-network.

International evidence suggests support during apprenticeships can work

Evaluating initiatives in this field is difficult because all those who seek support typically receive support. However, there is a great deal of variation within countries as to how initiatives are implemented. Available studies suggest that support for struggling apprentices can help promote successful completion. Studies of Australian apprentices found that the lack of support is a common cause of dropout. Having a credible third party that is available to apprentices facing personal problems or arguments in the workplace can reduce dropout (Snell and Hart, 2008[27]; Deloitte Access Economics, 2014[28]). Support directed to employers can also be very constructive. This may involve improving management capacity within firms so that employers are better able to deal with the challenges of integrating an apprentice into daily activities, training them and handling problems that arise. In Germany, the temporary suspension of mandatory training for apprentice supervisors led to an increase in dropout rates (BIBB, 2009[29]), which led to the re-introduction of the training requirement after a six-year suspension.

Conclusion

The question addressed in this chapter is how apprenticeships can be made to work for youth at risk of poor outcomes, being either out of education and employment or at risk of such a status. There is a solid basis to believe that apprenticeships can help make school-to-work transitions easier for such youth. While many countries offer employer subsidies to take on apprentices with weak academic profiles or from disadvantaged backgrounds, evidence of the efficacy of such financial incentives is unpersuasive. More effective are interventions designed to increase the speed with which a youth at risk apprentice can be expected to become a skilled, productive worker to cover the costs incurred by employers in their training. These include changes to the standard duration of an apprenticeship (either shorter or longer than is normally the case), preparatory programmes to help make a young person more attractive to an apprentice recruiter, or personalised support to tackle problems encountered by an apprentice whilst undertaking the apprenticeship.

References

Australian Government (2018), *Australian Apprenticeship Support Network*, http://www.australianapprenticeships.gov.au/australian-apprenticeship-support-network (accessed on 5 February 2018). [26]

Australian Government (2017), *Australian Apprenticeships*, http://www.australianapprenticeships.gov.au (accessed on 30 August 2017). [8]

Autorengruppe Bildungsberichterstattung (2016), *Bildung in Deutschland 2016 Ein indikatorengestützter Bericht mit einer Analyse zu Bildung und Migration Bildung in Deutschland 2016*, (Group of Writers on Educational Reporting, Education in Germany 2016: An Indicator-based Report with an Analysis Concerning Education and Migration in Germany, W. Bertelsmann Verlag, https://www.bildungsbericht.de/de/bildungsberichte-seit-2006/bildungsbericht-2016/pdf-bildungsbericht-2016/bildungsbericht-2016. [22]

BIBB (2009), "Ausbilder-Eignungsverordnung Vom 21 Januar 2009 ("Trainer aptitude regulations from 21 January 2009")", *Bundesgesetzblatt* 5, http://www.bibb.de/dokumente/pdf/ausbilder_eignungsverordnung.pdf. [29]

BMWFW (2016), *Lehrausbildung in verlängerter Lehrzeit und in Teilqualifikation*, (Extended Apprenticeship Training and Sub-qualification), Federal Ministry of Science, Research and Economy, http://www.bmwfw.gv.at/Berufsausbildung. [15]

Bonin, H. (2013), *Begleitforschung „Auswirkungen des Ausbildungsbonus auf den Ausbildungsmarkt und die öffentlichen Haushalte"*, (Accompanying Research "Impacts of the Training Bonus on the Training Market and Public Budgets"), Bundesministerium für Arbeit und Soziales, Berlin, http://www.bmas.de/SharedDocs/Downloads/DE/PDF-Publikationen/Forschungsberichte/fb438-Ausbildungsbonus-2013.pdf?__blob=publicationFile. [10]

Bonin, H. et al. (2010), *Vorstudie zur Evaluation von Fördermaßnahmen für Jugendliche im SGB II und SGB III*, (Preliminary Study on the Evaluation of Support Programmes for Young Adults, Codes of Social Law (SGB) II, III: Final Report), Centre for European Economic Research (ZEW), Ramboll and INFAS, http://www.bmas.de/SharedDocs/Downloads/DE/PDF-Publikationen/fb-fb405-evaluation-sgbII-sgbIII.pdf?__blob=publicationFile. [21]

Deloitte Access Economics (2014), *Australian Apprenticeships Mentoring Package Interim Evaluation*, Deloitte Access Economics, Barton, https://www.australianapprenticeships.gov.au/sites/ausapps/files/publication-documents/report_-_aamp_mentoring_package_interim_evaluation.pdf. [28]

Dornmayr, H. (2012), *Berufseinmündung von AbsolventInnen der Integrativen Berufsausbildung*, (Labour Market Entry of Graduates of Integrative Professional Training), Institute for Research on Qualifications and Training of the Austrian Economy, http://www.bmwfw.gv.at/Berufsausbildung/LehrlingsUndBerufsausbildung. [18]

Fuhrer, M. and J. Schweri (2010), "Two-year apprenticeships for young people with learning difficulties: a cost-benefit analysis for training firms", *Empirical Research in Vocational Education and Training*, Vol. 2/22, pp. 107-125. [14]

Gambin, L. and T. Hogarth (2016), "Factors affecting completion of apprenticeship training in England", *Journal of Education and Work*, Vol. 29/4, pp. 470-493, http://dx.doi.org/10.1080/13639080.2014.997679. [24]

Gelber, A., A. Isen and J. Kessler (2014), "The effects of youth employment: Evidence from New York City Summer Youth Employment Program Lotteries", *NBER Working Paper*, No. 20810, http://www.nber.org/papers/w20810. [3]

Heckman, J. and Y. Rubinstein (2001), "The importance of noncognitive skills: Lessons from the GED Testing Program", *The American Economic Review*, Vol. 91/2, pp. 145-149, http://jenni.uchicago.edu/papers/Heckman_Rubinstein_AER_2001_91_2.pdf. [4]

Heckman, J., J. Stixrud and S. Urzua (2006), "The effects of cognitive and noncognitive abilities on labor market outcomes and social behavior", *Journal of Labor Economics*, Vol. 24, pp. 411-482, http://www.nber.org/papers/w12006. [5]

Hofbauer, S., E. Kugi-Mazza and L. Sinowatz (2014), *Erfolgsmodell ÜBA: Eine Analyse der Effekte von Investitionen in die überbetriebliche Ausbildung ÜBA auf Arbeitsmarkt und öffentliche Haushalte*, (Success Model ÜBA: An Analysis of the Effects of Investments in External Vocational Training (ÜBA) fort he Labour Market and Public Budgets), WISO, Linz, http://www.isw linz.at/themen/dbdocs/LF_Hofbauer_Kugi_Sinow atz_03_14.pdf. [20]

Karmel, T. and D. Oliver (2011), *Pre-apprenticeships and their Impact on Apprenticeship Completion and Satisfaction*, National Centre for Vocational Education Research (NCVER), Adelaide, https://www.ncver.edu.au/publications/publications/all-publications/pre-apprenticeships-and-their-impact-on-apprenticeship-completion-and-satisfaction. [23]

Kis, V. (2016), "Work-based learning for youth at risk: Getting employers on board", *OECD Education Working Papers*, No. 150, OECD Publishing, Paris, http://dx.doi.org/10.1787/5e122a91-en. [19]

Mühlemann, S. (2016), "The cost and benefits of work-based learning", *OECD Education Working Papers*, No. 143, OECD Publishing, Paris, https://doi.org/10.1787/5jlpl4s6g0zv-en. [11]

Mühlemann, S., R. Braendli and S. Wolter (2013), "Invest in the best or compensate the weak? An empirical analysis of the heterogeneity of a firm's provision of human capita", *Evidence-based HRM: A Global Forum for Empirical Scholarship*, Vol. 1/1, pp. 80-95, http://www.emeraldinsight.com/doi/pdfplus/10.1108/20493981311318629. [13]

OECD (2015), *OECD Survey of Adult Skills (PIAAC) (Database 2012, 2015)*, http://www.oecd.org/site/piaac/publicdataandanalysis.htm. [6]

Quintini, G. and S. Martin (2014), "Same same but different: School-to-work transitions in emerging and advanced economies", *OECD Social, Employment and Migration Working Papers*, No. 154, OECD Publishing, Paris, https://doi.org/10.1787/5jzbb2t1rcwc-en. [1]

Sattar, S. (2010), "Evidence scan of work experience programs", *Mathematica Policy Research Reports*, No. 685b2a650bdf4437b1de31c2e, Mathematica Policy Research, Oakland, https://ideas.repec.org/p/mpr/mprres/685b2a650bdf4437b1de31c2e1c9c173.html. [2]

SBFI (2014), *Zweijährige Berufliche Grundbildung mit Eidgenössischem*, (Two-year Basic Education Culminating in a Federal Vocational Certificate), Swiss State Secretary for Education and Research, https://www.sbfi.admin.ch/dam/sbfi/de/dokumente/leitfaden_zweijaehrigeberuflichegrundbildungmiteidgenoessischemb.pdf.download.pdf/leitfaden_zweijaehrigeberuflichegrundbildungmiteidgenoessischemb.pdf. [17]

SDBB (2016), *EBA-Beruf – 2-jährige Lehre (EBA-Professions - Two-year Apprenticeship)*, (EBA-Professions - Two-year Apprenticeship), http://www.berufsberatung.ch. (accessed on 20 October 2016). [16]

Service-Public-Pro (2016), *Crédit d'impôt apprentissage*, https://www.service-public.fr/professionnels-entreprises/vosdroits/F31957. [9]

Snell, D. and A. Hart (2008), "Reasons for non-completion and dissatisfaction among apprentices and trainees: A regional case study", *International Journal of Training Research*, Vol. 6/1, https://www.tandfonline.com/doi/10.5172/ijtr.6.1.44. [27]

Stalder, B. and E. Schmid (2006), *Lehrvertragsauflösungen, ihre Ursachen und Konsequenzen. Ergebnisse aus dem Projekt LEVA*, (Cancellation of Apprenticeship Contracts - Causes and Consequences, Results of Project LEVA), https://www.be.ch/portal/de/veroeffentlichungen/publikationen.assetref/dam/documents/ERZ/GS/de/BiEv/ERZ_2006_Lehrvertragsaufloesungen_ihre_Ursachen_und_Konsequenzen.pdf. [25]

Wenzelmann, F. (2016), *Lessons from Subsidies in Germany: The Ausbildungsbonus*. [12]

Wirtschaftskammer Österreich (WKO) (2016), *Wirtschaftskammer Österreich*, (Austrian Chamber of Commerce), https://www.wko.at/service/foerderungen/integrative-berufsausbildung-und-teilqualifizierungen.html. [7]

Chapter 7. How to attract potential apprentices?

This chapter considers the attractiveness of apprenticeships to young people. It highlights the importance of programmes being genuinely attractive in terms of the prospects they offer, and also notes that apprenticeships are commonly poorly understood by young people. The chapter highlights the role of career guidance in tackling poor information, in challenging stereotypical thinking about apprenticeships, and in enabling school-to-work transitions. It presents insights from international literature on the characteristics of effective career guidance and the important role that employer engagement plays within it.

The statistical data for Israel are supplied by and under the responsibility of the relevant Israeli authorities. The use of such data by the OECD is without prejudice to the status of the Golan Heights, East Jerusalem and Israeli settlements in the West Bank under the terms of international law.

Issues and challenges

Among the many important decisions that young people must make, few are as important as those surrounding their educational choices and career aspirations. However, these important decisions are often strongly affected by gender, ethnicity and socio-economic factors. Young people commonly have an incomplete understanding of what apprenticeships have to offer and often fail to consider them at all. A strategic approach to career guidance can broaden career aspirations and ensure that decisions are made confidently on the basis of relevant and trustworthy information.

Choosing is hard

Education and training systems are often difficult to navigate, given the ever-growing number of options available to young people leading to very different career prospects. However, these decisions have long lasting consequences and effects. Evidence shows that the earnings that young people can expect following the completion of educational and training courses vary considerably by level, field/sector, and subject/occupation (Pfister, Sartore and Backes-Gellner, 2017[1]; Chevalier, 2011[2]).

Apprenticeships are not attractive in some countries

Many countries have issues in attracting potential apprentices. Students will not choose apprenticeships if they are seen as second choice options and/or dead ends where the opportunity to progress beyond an initial qualification is difficult. In some cases, apprenticeships are not of very high quality. Expected labour market outcomes, such as chances of getting a job and the wage level, are important. Apprenticeships are only as good as the success of their graduates: those that do not position students to succeed in the labour market and do not lead to further learning opportunities are, by definition, of poor quality. If apprenticeships are not attractive, it should be unsurprising that they struggle to attract young people. However, young people often have a very limited understanding of what an apprenticeship has to offer, and decisions made on the basis of ignorance are common. It is the task of career guidance to ensure that young people have an informed understanding of what it would be like to be an apprentice in different economic sectors.

Young people tend to have unrealistic and poorly informed expectations

There is a strong basis to believe that young people's career expectations are often unrealistic and poorly informed. Data from the Programme for International Student Assessment (PISA) 2015 show that most 15-year-olds have a clear view about what they want to do, and many are interested in just a small number of jobs: one-third of young people expected to work in just 10 different occupations [see (Musset and Mytna Kurekova, 2018[3]) for more data analysis].

Figure 7.1. Top 10 career expectations of 15-year-olds, in PISA 2015

Percentage of students who expressed career expectations in the different occupational categories, for students who responded

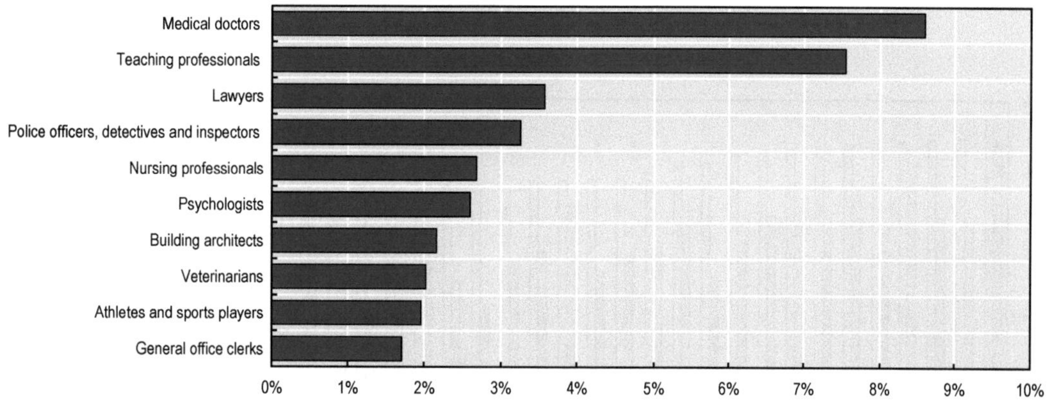

Note: Category medical practitioner/doctors formed by combining together medical doctors, specialist medical practitioners and generalist medical practitioner. Teaching professionals category created by combining all ISCO 23 (all categories together). Police officers, detectives and inspectors created by combining 5412, 3355 and 3411.
Source: OECD (2015[4]), PISA 2015 Database, www.oecd.org/pisa/data/2015database/.

StatLink http://dx.doi.org/10.1787/888933828524

Research shows that it is common for young people's career ambitions to be poorly aligned with actual labour market demand. Where teenagers' ambitions are unrealistic, long-term labour market penalties are to be expected (Yates, 2011[5]).

Family background, together with other characteristics, shape career thinking

Gender, ethnicity and migration background, and socio-economic factors all strongly shape career thinking. Analysis of PISA shows that young people from families enjoying higher socio-economic status (SES) are significantly more likely to want to work as professionals, and young people from families experiencing lower SES are significantly more likely to want to be technicians – even after statistical controls are put in place for their academic ability or proficiency levels (Musset and Mytna Kurekova, 2018[3]).

Figure 7.2. Advantaged students are more likely to want to work as professionals than more disadvantaged students

Percentage of students who say they want to work as professionals (ISCO category 2) by socio-economic status (SES)

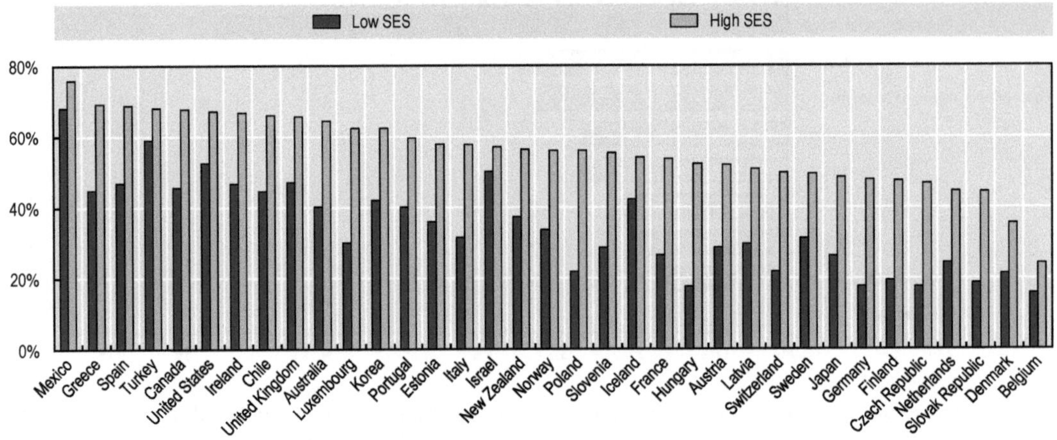

Note: Data is not available for the Slovak Republic. Occupations classified as professionals include, for example, civil engineers, secondary school teachers, medical practitioners, operating theatre nurses and computer systems analysts.
Source: OECD (2015[4]), PISA 2015 Database, www.oecd.org/pisa/data/2015database/.

StatLink http://dx.doi.org/10.1787/888933828543

Many young people do not automatically think about apprenticeships

Students often make career decisions with little knowledge of the labour market. Over recent years, as young people have stayed in education longer, career aspirations have also risen. Interest in highly skilled employment (as accessed through higher education) has risen considerably, while the percentage of young people wanting to work in a manual job (including skilled trades) or as a technician has fallen to less than one in twenty in some countries (Musset and Mytna Kurekova, 2018[3]).

Negative perceptions about some career paths, especially in the trades and in more technical fields, can discourage some students from engaging further in these fields. This means that many (and a growing number in some countries) young people may not even consider apprenticeships as an option. [See (Mann, 2016[6]) for evidence from England (United Kingdom).]

There are some important misconceptions about apprenticeships

Analysis of PISA data aligns with recent large-scale polling by the European Centre for the Development of Vocational Training (Cedefop, 2017[7]), and suggests that vocational education and training (VET), and the occupations to which it is a gateway, are often poorly understood. In 2017, CEDEFOP undertook an opinion survey on the image of VET across European Union countries. More than 35 000 people were interviewed. Results show that although VET suffers from a poor reputation compared to general education from those who have gone through general education, nine out of ten VET graduates were happy with their work skills. The survey shows huge misconceptions about VET itself: 70% believe that VET is simply about manual work, despite the diversity of jobs to which VET now leads. Regarding career guidance, only half of respondents from general education programmes said that they had received information about VET themselves before picking a programme (Cedefop, 2017$_{[7]}$).

Students and their parents may very well not be aware that apprenticeships are available in fields such as banking, the public sector and information and communication technology (ICT). In France, for example, one-third of all apprentices are at the post-secondary level. More than 50% of post-secondary apprentices are in services – notably in trade and administration[1] (OECD, 2014$_{[8]}$).

Students also may not be aware that there are opportunities to progress after pursuing an apprenticeship through diverse progression routes, some leading to management positions, others to owning and running a business, or to university programmes. Consequently, career guidance should be proactive, working with young people to explore different career paths. It cannot be taken for granted that young people properly understand apprenticeships. There is a strong case, consequently, for awareness raising campaigns like German VET week under the leadership of Federal President Steinmeier, or European Vocational Skills Week[2] in trying to influence the perceptions of young people and their influencers, notably parents. High profile skills competitions, such as WorldSkills,[3] and action to facilitate the international mobility of learners can play similar roles.

Gender may play a big role

Career aspirations are also heavily shaped by gender, with some important national variations. Within vocational education, apprenticeships and school-based programmes are often highly gendered. In general terms, girls have higher career expectations than boys, but these are often narrowly focused, for example in the medical professions and teaching. Girls also often turn away from science, technology, engineering and mathematics (STEM) professions. While research suggests that gender stereotyping can deter both girls and boys from pursuing specific careers, and that it can be countered by improved information, certain occupations appear so unfriendly to those not of the dominant gender that different approaches based on first-hand experiences are called for (OECD, 2015$_{[9]}$).

Quality matters in making apprenticeships attractive

Achieving high-quality and high-status apprenticeships requires the creation of a virtuous circle in which investment in the quality of a programme leads to strengthened labour market outcomes, which in turn attracts more high-ability candidates into the programme. This flow of high-ability students further improves the status of the programme and its attractiveness to employers, who will come to see it not only as high-quality education and training, but also as a means of recruiting able young students. This will further improve the labour market outcomes from the programme.

Policy argument 1: Apprentices need good generic skills

To ensure more equivalence with academic programmes, apprentices need to develop similar generic basic skills to those usually delivered in more academic programmes. This will provide the skills needed in jobs, a vital foundation for further progression into post-secondary education, including academic programmes, and will remove the risk that apprenticeship programmes are seen as dead ends. Permeability between vocational programmes and their general education equivalents, with clear pathways and avenues for progression between programmes and levels, make apprenticeships attractive.

Policy argument 2: Attractive apprenticeships attract attractive apprentices

As discussed above, the design and duration of apprenticeships influence the extent to which they are seen as attractive. Apprenticeships that are too long, and which include too great a proportion of unskilled labour, will struggle to attract more able students.

Career guidance is an essential feature of apprenticeship policy

Career guidance is both an individual and a social good: it helps individuals to progress in their learning and work, but it also helps the effective functioning of the labour and learning markets and contributes to a range of social policy goals, including social mobility and equity. This justifies public investment in career guidance activities.

Policy argument 1: Career guidance helps individuals to progress

Empirical evidence points towards career guidance services – both in and outside of school – as having a formative influence on young people's understanding of themselves and the world of work, and can often improve educational, social and economic outcomes (Hughes et al., 2016[10]).

Career guidance can help bring to the surface student preferences and inform students about education and work paths that they may not have already considered, or even know about. As a consequence, career guidance can support retention and a more efficient education system as students who choose programmes that prove not to suit them, either personally or academically, are less likely to succeed (OECD, 2012[11]).

How adolescents think about their futures in terms of career choices and education programmes has a significant impact on their lives as working adults. There are adult economic penalties linked to underestimating the length of education required to achieve aspirations – an indication of career confusion or unrealism. Such confusion is widespread. Commonly, young people who exhibit the most significant challenges in making informed decisions are from the most disadvantaged backgrounds, which raises significant questions of equity (Yates, 2011[5]).

Policy argument 2: Career guidance also helps the labour market to operate efficiently

Individuals with the right skills are more likely to be employed and, when in employment, tend to have better jobs. A skilled workforce also makes it easier to introduce and disseminate new technologies and work organisation practices, thereby boosting productivity and growth. To ensure that the skills acquired through the education and training system correspond to labour market needs, and hence avoid major issues with skill mismatch, it is important to develop stronger links between the world of education and the world of work. Career guidance and partnership activities play a major role in this. Indirectly, informed student choice exerts pressure on institutions to improve the quality of programmes (OECD, 2004[12]; OECD, 2012[11]; Hooley, 2015[13]).

Strategic use of career guidance will broaden aspirations and challenge stereotypes

Effective career guidance services have a positive influence on the educational and employment outcomes of young people (Hughes et al., 2016[10]). The question of what makes career guidance effective has been considered by the OECD and other researchers extensively over the last ten years (Musset and Mytna Kurekova, 2018[3]). Some of the commonplace challenges facing countries include the risks that career guidance is marginalised within school life, and that services are under-resourced and/or delivered by poorly trained staff who may lack objectivity and/or knowledge of the labour market (OECD, 2010[14]). PISA data show that it is often students who appear to have greatest need who have the least access to career guidance. For example, girls and students from low SES backgrounds often engage less frequently (Musset and Mytna Kurekova, 2018[3]).

Effective provision of career guidance should take into account the growing body of research literature and:

- Provide regular opportunities for young people from primary education onwards to reflect on the relationship between their educational experiences and their prospective futures.
- Allow students to consider the breadth of the labour market, particularly occupations of strategic economic importance and those that are newly emerging and/or likely to be misunderstood (such as skilled trades).
- Undertake school-wide approaches that not only engage career guidance specialists, but also teachers and school leaders, and parents.
- Systematically engage people in work and workplaces.
- Provide easy access to trustworthy labour market information and advice from well-trained, independent and impartial professionals in advance of key decision points.
- Challenge gender and ethnic stereotyping.
- Target young people from the most disadvantaged backgrounds for the greatest levels of intervention.

Policy argument 1: School-based career guidance must be comprehensive

Start early...

Even before starting school, children already have some awareness of jobs, which are linked to their personal experiences and family background. There is evidence that career-oriented activities should begin in primary school, or even earlier. These activities often aim simply to draw connections for children between education undertaken and possible future selves, in part to underpin engagement within schooling. This can also serve to challenge stereotypical perceptions of certain educational and career paths. For example, Primary Futures is a project developed by a non-profit charity in partnership with a range of stakeholders – government, employers, trade unions - in the United Kingdom that aims to bring people in work into primary schools to talk to students about their job and career route. In particular, it aims to expose children to the wide variety of roles that women can have in workplaces (Chambers et al., 2018[15]).

... and intervene at key transition points

Helping students understand their interests and aptitudes is important for further career planning and when making choices. The age and grade at which these choices are made vary greatly across OECD countries, depending on how and when tracking first occurs. These decisions can typically close education paths (OECD, 2012). This should mean, for example, that when students are choosing a school track, or a particular school or vocational programme, there should be a compulsory one-to-one interview with a career guidance professional.

Think school-wide approaches

Career guidance programmes are best implemented in ways that connect career learning to the curriculum, as opposed to isolated interventions, and with the support of the institution's leadership and wider partnerships (OECD, 2004[12]; Watts, 2009[16]). A comprehensive, all-encompassing multi-programme approach to career guidance has been developed by the Government of Prince Edward Island in Canada. The key elements include: career development integrated into health education in grades 1-9; compulsory career course in grade 10; experiential learning opportunities through a wide range of courses and programmes offered by the communities in school, and including hands-on experience out of school; partnerships with post-secondary institutions, employment specialists and industry sectors; specialised training to career guidance staff and teachers; and a parent coaching programme (ICCDPP, 2015[17]).

Integrate teachers too

There is a strong consensus in the literature that good quality career guidance requires the involvement of both qualified specialists and the wider teaching and school staff. Young people frequently seek out career support from a trusted adult within their immediate social network, and teachers are a likely source of this support, particularly where career aspirations are connected to interest in academic subjects. Teachers can and do link their subjects as taught in the curriculum to the world of work by, for example, highlighting how a particular scientific process is used in research or industry (Musset and Mytna Kurekova, 2018[3]).

Ensure that students can talk to well-trained career counsellors who are independent and impartial

Every student, whatever his/her personal background, needs to:

- Understand enough about career options to enable them to make informed decisions, whenever these decisions are open to them.
- Understand that choosing certain subjects and/or study programmes opens door to careers that would otherwise be closed.
- Understand enough about the world of work to know what skills, qualifications and attributes they need to succeed in it.

Well-trained career guidance counsellors can help provide young people with these three elements by relating objective careers information to the personal circumstances of students. Career guidance responsibilities are demanding and important: the assimilation of the guidance profession into psychological counselling, as is sometimes the case in OECD countries, distorts and marginalises this role. While it makes sense to deliver guidance in schools in order to ensure access to all students, it is important that guidance professionals preserve their independence from the school. This could involve, for example, a professional career guidance service managed from outside schools, but with a roving function in schools (OECD, 2010[14]).

Independent career advisers – in and out of school – can help students in different ways: through questionnaires and tests they can help them understand their interests and preferences better; they can inform students about jobs that could match their preferences and interests, and the paths to reach these jobs; and they can help broaden students' horizons and present them with new and different options than just the few well-known professions, such as those accessed through apprenticeships. PISA 2012 analysis from Canada shows that only 8% of students plan on pursuing a job in the traditional trades. However, those who have researched information about these trades, had undertaken an internship, or had been encouraged by their parents were much more likely to plan to pursue a job in a traditional trade.

Policy argument 2: School-based services should be complemented with opportunities given by ICT and labour market information

The spread of ICT has opened up new forms of career guidance, such as self-service and the use of technology and social media in providing and presenting career guidance information. It is a vehicle for ensuring that young people have access to information on:

- All available options and pathways specific to an individual's needs, including VET options.
- The qualifications to which the options lead, and the further qualifications to which they give access.
- The occupations to which these qualifications provide access.
- The labour market outcomes achieved by those successfully completing the programmes, including the nature of their jobs, their salary/wage levels and projected demand for the occupation.

In the case of jobs in an occupational sector directly related to VET programmes, it is important to know the extent to which skills and competences acquired in the programme are used in work.

For example, Utdanning.no[4] is a public career guidance web portal in Norway. It includes an overview of the educational pathways in Norway, where the education is being provided, and descriptions of more than 600 careers and professions. The webpage also includes interviews with skilled workers, overviews of places to work, and information on average salary. A similar tool, developed in Canada, Job Bank,[5] is also available as a mobile phone application.

Policy argument 3: Young people with the greatest need demand the greatest attention

Providing objective and reliable career information and varied exposure to different workplaces – through practices such as career talks, job shadowing and mentoring programmes which allow personal contact with employers and professionals – to all students can help reduce the influence of informal and less objective sources of information (such as parents and friends).

Disadvantaged students commonly need help overcoming obstacles to pursuing their education and to make fulfilling career choices. Programmes specifically for disadvantaged students, such as those at risk of dropping out, work best when they are targeted, located in the community and highly individualised. To mitigate gender stereotypes that can prevent girls progressing in the same fields as boys, schools can help students cultivate a wider perspective on different career options, including in traditional VET fields, through better career information and regular career talks and workplace visits. In Canada, the Futures in Skilled Trades and Technology Programme supports the greater participation of women in skilled trades in the Newfoundland and Labrador Province by piloting modules targeted at girls in primary school. The Ontario Youth Apprenticeship Programme reserves some of its funding to promote skilled trades among women through career talks and hands-on activities (OECD, 2015[9]).

In the case of students with an immigrant background, barriers can be both objective (i.e. language proficiency), cultural (i.e. poor reputation of an occupation or educational pathway in an originating country), or social (i.e. lack of first-hand contacts in important economic areas, such as apprenticeship employers). Such students, and their parents, might easily lack sufficient information about the education system and career paths in a new institutional context. Some countries, consequently, have specific initiatives to inform students with a migrant background and their parents about vocational options.

Effective career guidance strategies demand close co-operation between schools and the world of work

To make properly informed decisions, students need to have a good picture of work and where they need to put their efforts while still in education in order to be able to realise their dreams. To achieve this, schools should encourage first-hand understanding of the world of work from the earliest years.

Career guidance activities should fully integrate diverse members of the economic community into their career guidance services, ensuring multiple and authentic interactions with young people from an early age. Action should be taken to identify and address obstacles preventing engagement. Where countries are new to employer engagement, it is best to begin where logistics are easiest. In terms of delivery, countries and schools should consider that:

- Employer/employee talks and career fairs are a relatively easy and effective tool.
- ICT can provide many new ways of facilitating the interactions between schools and employers (Musset and Mytna Kurekova, 2018[3]).

Policy argument 1: There are many benefits linked to engaging those in work with career guidance for young people

In many countries, schools have long engaged people in work in aspects of education, for example, in careers fairs and talks, as job shadows and the hosts of work placements and visits, and as enterprise champions and mentors. Volunteer employers and workers are an information resource for young people whose own networks are inherently limited. The engagement of people who have first-hand knowledge of workplaces offers young people something additional to the professional advice offered by career guidance services. It allows trusted insights into expressions of working life, which can provide young people with new and useful information about the world of work – and how it relates to their own individual sense of who they are and who they might become.

While research literature remains limited, a growing body of research has investigated and demonstrated significant links between such engagement and the employment (as well as educational) outcomes of young people [see for example (Kashefpakdel and Percy, 2016[18])].

This engagement can be particularly effective in challenging negative assumptions about specific careers, as former apprentices can speak with authority to students about what a particular path is really like. In Scotland (United Kingdom), for example, former apprentices, and employers who participate in the apprenticeship programme, routinely go into schools to promote the flagship apprenticeship programme (Skills Development Scotland (SDS), 2015[19]).

It is important that young people have the opportunity to engage with people working across a wide range of occupations, as each will bring their own perspective on what it means to work in a particular profession.

And what is there in it for employers? They too are often interested in providing students in school with knowledge about jobs and the workplace for a range of reasons, including: shaping the future skills supply (particularly in areas where there are critical shortages); the opportunity to promote careers within their organisation or sector; the opportunity to "try before they buy"; and to meet young people who they may be interested in employing; and to help enhance young people's employability skills so that they become more effective employees (Mann, Rehill and Kashefpakdel, 2018[20]).

There are significant variations between countries

Available PISA data show a significant variation between countries in the extent to which young people engage with employers as part of the career guidance they receive. On average, students are less likely to engage in activities involving employers than in wholly school-based activities: fewer than 30% of PISA respondents, on average, had visited a job fair by the age of 15 (Musset and Mytna Kurekova, 2018[3]).

Participation levels tend to be greater when countries have strong programmes of vocational education, with VET students being much more likely, for example, to have completed an internship.

How schools can efficiently and effectively draw on people in work

Employers and schools often face technical, legal or information barriers that might deter them from mutual co-operation. Employers have enterprises to run and might not have sufficient motivation to engage in the provision of career guidance, and it is not always clear for employers how they can benefit from participating in career guidance activities. Schools may lack resources to cover the costs linked to reaching out to people in work.

Different types of activities come with different transactional costs. Mentoring programmes are, for example, demanding for both employers and schools to administer. Careers talks and careers fairs are much less demanding and have been evidenced to provide young people with positive outcomes (Mann, Rehill and Kashefpakdel, 2018[20]). They make an excellent starting point for countries and schools without a tradition of such engagement. For governments, the most important task is to make it easy for people in work to become involved by addressing barriers preventing engagement. Online platforms can facilitate high volume and low cost employer engagement in education. For schools, it is important that they are supported in the process of exposing students to the world of work.

Like career guidance, exposure to the world of work can serve to challenge or replicate patterns of social reproduction. Research suggests that schools should focus on the quantity (numbers of interactions) and quality (student perceptions of usefulness) of provision and target action particularly at students from families which lack strong social networks related to careers of interest.

Other stakeholders, such as trade unions, are also important means of enabling schools to access people in work who have valuable insights to share with young people. Danish VET students, for example, act as role models and visit lower secondary schools to promote VET through "The Route to VET", a campaign initiated and led by the Danish Vocational and Technical School Students Union (Erhvervsskolernes ElevOrganisation (EEO), 2015[21]). At school visits, young role models present their own experiences on why they chose VET, their training and the possibilities they have both within the labour market and for further education. The campaign reflects a partnership between VET schools, employers and lower secondary schools to increase first-hand encounters between younger students and older peers able to provide personal insight into VET pathways.

Conclusion

This chapter explores how to attract young people's interest in apprenticeship. It is a particularly pertinent question in the many countries where apprenticeships have not appeared to be attractive options. If apprenticeships are to be successful, they must be able to attract able and ambitious young people. They will only do this if they offer a genuine gateway into skilled employment. Where the quality of apprenticeships is poor, young people will vote with their feet. Students and their families often have a weak understanding of what apprenticeships actually have to offer. This is particularly the case where they have become available across a wide range of occupations at different skills levels. It is the task of career guidance to ensure that young people make informed decisions at the right time. Evidence from the PISA database has shown how career aspirations are shaped by gender, socio-economic status and migrant background. These aspirations rarely reflect labour market demand. There is an onus on schools to take a proactive and strategic approach to career guidance that begins young, broadens ambitions, and ensures that regular encounters with independent and well-trained career guidance professionals are the norm. Essential to effective guidance is giving young people the chance to find out for themselves, through activities such as career talks and job shadowing, what it is like to follow different occupational and learning pathways, including apprenticeships.

Notes

[1] For comparison, three out of four apprentices at the upper-secondary level were in technical and industrial fields that same period (mainly in civil engineering and in construction).

[2] More information about the European Vocational Skills Week can be found at: https://ec.europa.eu/social/vocational-skills-week/evsw2018_en.

[3] More information about WorldSkills can be found at: www.worldskills.org/.

[4] More information can be found at: www.utdanning.no.

[5] More information can be found at: www.jobbank.gc.ca.

References

Cedefop (2017), *Cedefop European Public Opinion Survey on Vocational Education and Training*, Publications Office of the European Union, Luxembourg. [7]

Chambers, N. et al. (2018), *Drawing the Future: Exploring the Career Aspirations of Primary School Children from Around the World*, Education and Employers, London, https://www.educationandemployers.org/wp-content/uploads/2018/01/Drawing-the-Future-FINAL-REPORT.pdf. [15]

Chevalier, A. (2011), "Subject choice and earnings of UK graduates", *Economics of Education Review*, Vol. 30, pp. 1187-1201. [2]

Erhvervsskolernes ElevOrganisation (EEO) (2015), *Kampagnen*, (Campaigns), http://eeo.dk/vejentil/om-kampagnen. [21]

Hooley, T. (2015), *The Economic Benefits of Career Guidance*, Careers England. [13]

Hughes, D. et al. (2016), *Careers Education: International Literature Review*, Education Endowment Foundation, London, https://educationendowmentfoundation.org.uk/evidence-summaries/evidence-reviews/careers-education/. [10]

ICCDPP (2015), *ICCDPP 2015 Symposium. Promising/Best Practices: Canada*, ICCDPP, http://www.is2015.org/wp-content/uploads/2015/06/Canada-Promising-Practices-Panel-2-2.pdf. [17]

Kashefpakdel, E. and C. Percy (2016), "Career Education that Works: An economic analysis using the British Cohort Study", *Journal of Education and Work*, Vol. 30/3, pp. 217-234, https://doi.org/10.1080/13639080.2016.1177636. [18]

Mann, A. (2016), "Promoting apprenticeships to young people and schools", in Way, D. (ed.), *A Race to the Top: Achieving Three Million More Apprenticeships by 2020*, Winchester University Press, Winchester. [6]

Mann, A., J. Rehill and E. Kashefpakdel (2018), *Employer Engagement in Education: Insights from International Evidence for Effective Practice and Future Research*, Education and Employers Research, London, https://www.educationandemployers.org/research/employerengagementineducation/. [20]

Musset, P. and L. Mytna Kurekova (2018), "Working it out: Career guidance and employer engagement", *OECD Education Working Papers*, No. 175, OECD Publishing, Paris, http://dx.doi.org/10.1787/51c9d18d-en. [3]

OECD (2015), *PISA 2015 Database*, http://www.oecd.org/pisa/data/2015database/. [4]

OECD (2015), *The ABC of Gender Equality in Education: Aptitude, Behaviour, Confidence*, PISA, OECD Publishing, Paris, http://dx.doi.org/10.1787/9789264229945-en. [9]

OECD (2014), *Skills beyond School: Synthesis Report*, OECD Reviews of Vocational Education and Training, OECD Publishing, Paris, http://dx.doi.org/10.1787/9789264214682-en. [8]

OECD (2012), *Equity and Quality in Education: Supporting Disadvantaged Students and Schools*, OECD Publishing, Paris, http://dx.doi.org/10.1787/9789264130852-en. [11]

OECD (2010), *Learning for Jobs*, OECD Reviews of Vocational Education and Training, OECD Publishing, Paris, https://doi.org/10.1787/9789264087460-en. [14]

OECD (2004), *Career Guidance and Public Policy: Bridging the Gap*, OECD Publishing, Paris, http://dx.doi.org/10.1787/9789264105669-en. [12]

Pfister, C., S. Sartore and U. Backes-Gellner (2017), "The relative importance of type of education and subject area: Empirical evidence for educational decisions", *Evidence-based HRM: A Global Forum for Empirical Scholarship*, Vol. 5/1, pp. 30-58, https://www.emeraldinsight.com/doi/full/10.1108/EBHRM-05-2015-0019. [1]

Skills Development Scotland (SDS) (2015), *Equalities Action Plan for Modern Apprenticeships in Scotland*, Skills Development Scotland, Glasgow, https://www.skillsdevelopmentscotland.co.uk/media/40691/2869_sds_equalities_action_plan_digital_v7.pdf. [19]

Watts, A. (2009), *The Relation of Career Guidance to VET*, OECD Publishing, Paris, http://www.oecd.org/education/skills-beyond-school/44246616.pdf. [16]

Yates, S. (2011), "Early occupational aspirations and fractured transitions: A study of entry into 'NEET' status in the UK", *Journal of Social Policy*, Vol. 40/3, pp. 513-534. [5]

Annex A. Apprentices and apprenticeship graduates in the Survey of Adult Skills (PIAAC)

Current apprentices

Current apprentices are defined as currently studying in upper-secondary education or short post-secondary programmes (at ISCED level 3 longer than two years, or ISCED 4C) and defining themselves as apprentices or holding an apprentice contract. Variables C_Q07 and D_Q09 from the background questionnaire for the Survey of Adult Skills, a product of the Programme for the International Assessment of Adult Competencies (PIAAC), were used to identify current apprentices. As these variables do not distinguish between internships and apprenticeships, apprenticeships have been limited to programmes leading to upper -secondary and short post-secondary programmes only, with the assumption that internships are more common in long post-secondary programmes than at lower levels of education and training (Kuczera, 2017[1]).

Apprenticeship graduates

In Austria, Canada and Germany, individuals were classified as apprenticeship graduates if they identified "apprenticeship" as their highest qualification (question B_Q01aAT in Austria, B_Q01aCA6 in Canada, and B_Q01aDE2_REC in Germany in the national background questionnaires for the Survey of Adults Skills). In Norway, an apprenticeship graduate is a person whose highest qualification is ISCED 3C (lasting for two years or more) (question B_Q01a in the background questionnaire for the Survey of Adult Skills). In Denmark, an apprenticeship graduate is a person whose highest qualification is at upper-secondary level (ISCED 3, of two years or more) and the qualification was obtained in one of the following areas of study: social science, business and law, science, mathematics and computing, teacher training and education science, engineering, manufacturing and construction (questions B_Q01a and B_Q01b in the background questionnaire for the Survey of Adult Skills) (Kuczera, 2017[1]).

Reference

Kuczera, M. (2017), "Incentives for apprenticeship", *OECD Education Working Papers*, No. 152, OECD Publishing, Paris, http://dx.doi.org/10.1787/55bb556d-en. [1]

ORGANISATION FOR ECONOMIC CO-OPERATION AND DEVELOPMENT

The OECD is a unique forum where governments work together to address the economic, social and environmental challenges of globalisation. The OECD is also at the forefront of efforts to understand and to help governments respond to new developments and concerns, such as corporate governance, the information economy and the challenges of an ageing population. The Organisation provides a setting where governments can compare policy experiences, seek answers to common problems, identify good practice and work to co-ordinate domestic and international policies.

The OECD member countries are: Australia, Austria, Belgium, Canada, Chile, the Czech Republic, Denmark, Estonia, Finland, France, Germany, Greece, Hungary, Iceland, Ireland, Israel, Italy, Japan, Korea, Latvia, Lithuania, Luxembourg, Mexico, the Netherlands, New Zealand, Norway, Poland, Portugal, the Slovak Republic, Slovenia, Spain, Sweden, Switzerland, Turkey, the United Kingdom and the United States. The European Union takes part in the work of the OECD.

OECD Publishing disseminates widely the results of the Organisation's statistics gathering and research on economic, social and environmental issues, as well as the conventions, guidelines and standards agreed by its members.

OECD PUBLISHING, 2, rue André-Pascal, 75775 PARIS CEDEX 16
(91 2018 14 1 P) ISBN 978-92-64-30647-9 – 2018

Printed by Libri Plureos GmbH in Hamburg,
Germany

9 789264 306479